Quick and Creative Art Projects for Creative
Therapists with (Very) Limited Budgets

Quick and Creative Art Projects for Creative Therapists with (Very) Limited Budgets

RACHEL BRANDOFF
and
ANGEL THOMPSON

Jessica Kingsley *Publishers*
London and Philadelphia

First published in 2019
by Jessica Kingsley Publishers
73 Collier Street
London N1 9BE, UK
and
400 Market Street, Suite 400
Philadelphia, PA 19106, USA

www.jkp.com

Library of Congress Cataloging in Publication Data
Names: Brandoff, Rachel, author. | Thompson, Angel (Angel Louise), 1972-
author.
Title: Quick and creative art projects for creative therapists with (very)
limited budgets / Rachel Brandoff and Angel Thompson.
Description: London ; Philadelphia : Jessica Kingsley Publishers, 2019. |
Includes bibliographical references.
Identifiers: LCCN 2018039536 | ISBN 9781785927942
Subjects: LCSH: Art therapy.
Classification: LCC RC489.A7 B73 2019 | DDC 616.89/1656--
dc23 LC record available at https://lccn.loc.gov/2018039536

British Library Cataloguing in Publication Data
A CIP catalogue record for this book is available from the British Library

ISBN 978 1 78592 794 2
eISBN 978 1 78450 787 9

Printed and bound by CPI Group (UK) Ltd, Croydon, CR0 4YY

Contents

Introduction

Why are we writing this book?

We are aware that there is no shortage out there of books, how-to manuals, and other tools for art direction, inspiring ideas, and creativity. We own many and can personally attest to their usefulness as resources. We love consulting books for art ideas to use with clients, either directly or as jumping-off points. In that way our book is a homage to those that came before, merged with a mindfulness regarding material costs and availability. We were both fortunate enough to work for an organization that had a substantial materials budget and a wealth of well-stocked shelves with neat rows of paint, paper, brushes, clay, drawing supplies, pom-poms, googly eyes, and hundreds of other useful supplies, more than a lay person would be able to name. More often we have been in the exact opposite position, being charged with creating an art activity, workshop, exhibition, or program, with next to nothing, the desired materials list greatly exceeding the meager budget allowed. And so we have become magicians, networkers, and scavengers, bent on sourcing supplies in the service of clients.

We as art therapists and teaching artists frequently need new ideas to keep things fresh for clients, students, and also for ourselves. When we first proposed doing a session like this at the Expressive Therapies Summit[1] in 2016, colleagues were eager to attend;

---

1   www.expressivetherapiessummit.com

in fact, the session filled up pretty quickly. Professional colleagues and attendees at our session told us that they needed new ideas that were treatment-oriented, but that did not require them to drop a ton of money on fancy art supplies. We regularly heard tales (and have our own similar stories!) about administrators and bosses with lofty expectations of the art that would be produced and the creativity that would be a bragging right for the organization. Of course, time and again the stories had the same current: I was told to move mountains and given no budget.

So we write this book to give you great ideas for home-run projects that necessitate little art materials or budget, and in some cases recycled art materials. We have been frustrated by the volume of pictures online that do not come with instructions and the projects with huge materials lists that can't be easily simplified. There is a time to creatively try your own new ideas, but sometimes having something tried and true is most useful. It can be hard for busy professionals to find time to bring newly created ideas to their work.

Using pre-designed projects still allows for spontaneity in therapeutic and educational environments. Spontaneity is valuable and we don't want to minimize its importance or discourage its use. You may start with a fantastic plan, only to then abandon it based on an emergent session content or situation, or if something else simply needs to take precedence. Even in these cases, having a plan in mind or a project at the ready can contribute to flow. A well-planned art project allows you to be more available to the participants and any emotional or psychological issues that come up spontaneously. We strongly believe that having a premeditated project doesn't make you a scripted teacher or therapist, just a prepared one.

Our aim is that the ideas and projects contained herein will contribute to your arsenal of tools in working with your community. We hope this book will become your useful go-to for fun projects, for sourcing material ideas, and for using your limited budget in the most efficient way.

Is this book for you? (It probably is!)

We have written this book for people who see a value to bringing the arts and creativity to the people they serve within the work that they do. You may be a creative arts therapist, social worker, community leader, activities coordinator, educator, teaching artist, or other mental health, social service, or helping professional. Perhaps you already integrate arts and creativity into your work, and need fresh ideas, or perhaps you've been itching to bring in art directives, but have been at a loss as to where to start. Either way, we believe that you will find this book useful.

Along with our art projects, we have included useful strategies, creative ways to access and use materials, and leading questions for discussion and opening up a dialogue about what is being generated in a creative process. No book can give you expertise that comes from practice, but ours will give you ideas to take into your classroom, therapy session, or group art making as you hone your own expertise. We have packed it full of ideas readily accessed, whether you need a jumping-off point for your own directives or a lesson plan, from warm-up to reflection, that can be done with little customization.

If you are a teacher, therapist, social worker, or counselor, and you are expecting your clients or students to make art, we encourage you yourself to make art also (on your own, if not with them). We encourage you to run into the challenges of the creative process—artist's block, self-criticism and inner judgment, confusion and uncertainty about how to take initiative. It is through experiencing the perils of creativity, in part, that you learn how to overcome these obstacles and give yourself creative license. It is by experiencing this creative journey first hand that you will better be able to lead someone else on their journey. Giving oneself the freedom to create takes courage, commitment, motivation, but not (as it turns out) a ton of money, and we'll explore that here too!

How to use this book

If you are a seasoned facilitator of art directives in a clinical, social, or education environment, then you may have already engaged in some projects like these. We hope that you'll find something new in our project variations and alternatives, or in resources, or possibly in a money-saving tip. Even the most experienced facilitators can sometimes benefit from a boost of ideas or creative energy; we know this from experience!

If you are a novice, then have fun exploring our ideas in a project book format. We hope that this will give you support and structure as you begin to implement art activities with clients or students.

As you work in art facilitation, make sure that you seek out the appropriate training, supervision, and qualifications. Everyone starts somewhere and no one is born with experience, but at the same time, it could be unethical to work beyond your scope of practice or education. An honest assessment and presentation of skills builds a principled practice.

We urge you to use the ideas in this book as a springboard into the work that you do. To that end, it is not likely that any project will be perfect for your setting and participants as it is. You will likely need to adapt activities for your own use with clients. We have tried to help with this process by being broad and inclusive in our suggestion of goals, approaches, and resources. There are specific things that we recommend considering when adapting these ideas to your work, such as:

- *Client issues:* This includes all of the things about your client, such as their age, developmental stage, comfort level with art materials and creative expression, preferences, aversions, strengths, weaknesses, diagnoses, treatment goals and objectives, and stage of treatment or development of the relationship.

- *Time:* This includes the amount of time and sessions for art making, for material exploration, and for processing of relevant content.

- *Space:* This includes the features and parameters of your space, as well as limitations on materials, furniture, privacy, client art storage space, mess, materials storage, and transport.

- *Materials:* Considerations here include what you have available, what you can find, and what you want to use and can tie to therapeutic or educational goals for your client or student. A budget ceiling is also important to consider as well as what you should spend your limited budget on.

- *Other:* Here we include outside influences such as academic curriculum, organizational mission, parameters of grant funders, or regulations of credentialing bodies. Considerations might include deadlines that pertain to an art exhibition or sharing.

We know that there are so many things to consider when tailoring an activity to your own clients that we have even built and included in this text a reference sheet of *Customization considerations,* which you can find as Appendix 2.

Remember that your students or clients are individuals, and not every activity works well for each person or group of people. You will always have a better "sell" on an activity that you like and appreciate, but just because you like it does not mean that your client will also. Remain open and flexible to the possibility that you may have to improvise or scrap an idea at the last minute.

Part of being creative with no budget means pushing yourself to make something out of nothing. It requires that you be a waste management advocate, a community-oriented consumer, and a passionate recycler. It can be as easy to be creative with no money as it can be with lots of money, although it may require more passion or planning. We have found that building art with little or no budget results in a thoughtful product that validates our creativity and sense of inventiveness. Just as our clients and students have their esteem raised with the verification of themselves as inventors, so too do we.

Issues of equality

Providing methods and access to art and art making that are not financially dependent promotes equality in our society. Art making should not be just in the domain of those with the means to purchase high-end materials, instruction, and exposure.

Educators and therapists are frequently charged with providing access to the arts and to culture through the arts. We can do this with big impact and little money. In 2007, while working for a community arts organization, we wrote a recycling-based arts curriculum that was highly popular and versatile. Using trash to make treasures, and having quality art out of recycled material, was a way of being creative but also of raising awareness about ecology and environmental issues. A by-product of this initiative was the proverbial leveling of the playing field. Waste, recycling, and the environment touched everybody's life. In this program, art did too, so it felt like a universal value.

There are significant resources concerning equality in the arts centering on issues of physical disability, but the arts have limitations in many respects. Financial accessibility is an issue in both art making and art appreciation. Many museums now offer a free day, or a pay-what-you-can option, but art making too often remains in the domain of those with disposable income.

In an effort to better learn who is currently engaging in arts and cultural opportunities, Great Art and Culture for Everyone, Arts Council England (ACE), a British organization, shared information that clearly states that "parents from higher socio-economic groups are significantly more likely to take their children to arts events and to encourage them to participate in arts activities." They also found that younger children are more likely to engage in art than older children, girls more than boys, and there are differences in the amount of arts engagement between ethnic groups (Thorpe 2017).

Art is something that everyone can benefit from. We are strong proponents of everyone having access to that benefit. To this end, we dream of a culture that might promote equality and art making through civic art material budgets or expanded social status associated with the use of recycled material. We hope that by encouraging the use of non-traditional art materials, or things found outside of the art supply store, we also encourage incremental steps towards accessibility of art for all.

Anything can be art

We believe so fervently in the benefits of creative applications in therapy, as well as in healthcare and education, that we refuse to allow paltry issues such as a lack of budget, space, or materials interfere with the projects that can be made. We support the outstanding efforts of artists (sometimes called eco artists, and sometimes avant-garde) who embrace found objects, nature objects, trash, and recycled materials, and endorse this as a way of thinking about and approaching art making in the therapeutic and educational realms. Art can help raise our awareness about phenomena both inside and outside of ourselves (Al-Banna 2017; Callaway n.d.; Falcon n.d.; Jones 2013; Webster 2012).

Trash, recycled, or found objects play well to the metaphor of people who are marginalized, discarded, or on the fringes of society. Moreover, these metaphors play well to the universality of feelings such as loneliness, rejection, lack of inclusion, or being different, which seem to impact all people at some point in life, regardless of station, status, or resources. Construction in art validates our sense of self as creative beings, and lets us confidently affirm *I am*!

Create, explore, and grow!

PROJECTS

In this section we present five chapters that discuss different projects, which we have conceived of as broad project categories: masks, flags, boxes, charms, talismans, amulets, and books and journals. In addition to some discussion about these ideas as a type of project, we give several art techniques that may vary in material or approach for the projects. We make an effort to distinguish between required and recommended materials where possible, knowing that if all you have are the bare essentials of materials, you could still make a really inspired piece of art. We also give ideas for project goals, related warm-ups, how to present your project to participants, project background or historical relevance, project preparation, and ideas for questions, discussion, and wrapping up your art-making session. In some places you'll note that we discuss applicable cultural issues and provide additional resources.

Warm-ups

We are huge fans of warm-ups that can help to center clients and facilitators, and allow all participants to acknowledge what they are bringing into the room, group, or therapeutic space. We describe warm-ups to participants as an opportunity to "take stock of the emotional and psychic baggage that we are carrying, and to assess how heavy it is at this particular time." Use of warm-ups helps participants to prepare to be in the space, to connect with others, and to take healthy and calculated risks. Warm-ups can foster spontaneity, focus, and engagement in both individuals and groups. They promote trust and cohesion of group members in the service of common goals.

Appreciation vs. appropriation: Note of intention

Borrowing symbols and styles from different cultures and using them for inspiration in art is an age-old tradition. In fact, it likely explains how some symbols appear in various forms in a variety of different traditions and cultures: "Artisans have always learned their trade by copying their predecessors, picking up a pen, brush, or chisel first to imitate, then to reinvent" (Seltzer 2008, p.36). At the same time it is nearly impossible to extricate the sharing of techniques and aesthetics from the context of the political and cultural history under which they occurred:

> ...consider his masterpiece 'Les Demoiselles D'Avignon', which is famed for its incorporation of African masks. Picasso had seen African masks in several museums in Paris, and was intrigued by their formal and spiritual qualities. What complicates this matter is that it was the context of colonial exploitation that brought African art into the domain of French culture, and made Picasso's interaction with these masks possible. (Millington 2017, para. 6)

In our modern world there is a lot of discussion about what is considered cultural appropriation, and when or if it is appropriate to include cultural symbols or aesthetics by people not of that culture. Appropriation carries the connotation of exploitation and dominance that is intrinsically tied to the history between cultures. Without recognition of the origins and the potential complexities associated with that culture and with one's own, there is, indeed, risk of offense. Some people deem this risk so certain that they feel that the use of another culture's symbols or distinct aesthetics is both offensive and wrong.

While we agree that cultural influence in art, including the use of distinctive features, has the potential to be disrespectful or marginalizing, we believe that it can be done in a way that is appropriate, respectful, and reverent. Artists are frequently inspired by what they see and learn, and we want to encourage people to learn about cultures other than their own. We believe that clarification of intention and education of origin are two key ingredients that can help the use of symbols and styles to be honored and celebrated. Art that is born of respectful cultural exchange can broaden horizons.

Materials: Essentials and alternatives

Working within the constraints of a budget often means making the materials you have access to work for the project you have planned. With this in mind, we have designed projects that require few but accommodate many materials. Essential materials can usually be pared down to a form/structure base, tools, adhesives, and items for decoration or personalizing, the latter being the category with the most flexibility.

There are some materials that are dependent on others. They are for the most part logical connections. If you are painting, you will also need brushes and containers for water. If you are stitching, you will need needles or a hole punch and masking tape to create an aglet on the tip of the string for hand stitching. Keep in mind that you will also need to adjust the adhesives you offer based on the materials they work best with.

WHAT GLUE SHOULD I USE?

Glue sticks are best for adhering paper to paper and light-weight porous materials such as feathers; they have a quick drying time.

White glue is best for light to mediumweight porous materials such as cardboard; it requires some drying time.

Tacky glue is best for securing heavier items like wood pieces or those with low porosity, such as gems. It also works well for fabric and notions; it requires significant drying time.

Hot glue/glue guns are best for low or no porosity items or odd-shaped mixed media, such as little toys, stones, and tulle; it has a very quick cooling time.

Decoupage medium is best for adhering a lightweight material such as paper to a low or nonporous surface such as glass or plastic; it requires some drying time but can be painted before it is completely dry.

Chapter 1

Masks

Purpose

Masks are used for a variety of reasons across cultures, ranging from protective disguise to entertainment and performance. Mask making and wearing allows a person to try out a new identity, or practice for the identity that they hope to wear. Mask making can allow for a proverbial stepping into another's shoes, and as such is a great tool for building empathy and insight.

Masks are frequently used in the realms of education and art therapy, since they are great tools for helping us to examine and learn more about ourselves and about others. Masks can be created in a variety of different ways and with different materials, which may depend in part on available time, material and financial resources, and physical and developmental abilities of participants. Simple or elaborate mask projects can be developed using cardboard, prefabricated plastic, paper pulp, or cardstock mask forms, paper plates or bags, papier-mâché, air-dry clay, or plaster strips. With a significant budget, you could purchase plaster strips so that a participant could make a mask that is literally sculpted from their own face. Plastic mask forms are cheaper, and foil or paper plates are cheaper still. Recycled milk or water jugs, as used in Project 2, can be collected for free.

GENERAL HISTORY OF MASKS

Utilitarian use: Masks have played an important part in many cultures throughout the ages. They have been used for protection from diseases, in the military, and in sports. Perhaps the earliest use of masks was in connection with hunting (Dall 1884). Early Stone Age men would wear "disguise masks" to stalk their prey, and later use the mask to house the animal's spirit in the hope of appeasing the animal for giving its life so that the man and his family could survive.

Festival and theatrical use: Masks have always been part of festive celebrations like Halloween, Mardi Gras, Purim, Carnivale, Chinese New Year, and "masked balls" known as masquerade balls. The disguise is intended to create comic characters, to cause humorous confusion, or to help a prankster achieve anonymity. Throughout Europe, Latin America, and Africa masks are associated with folk festivals, especially those held around seasonal changes or around the beginning and end of a year. Universally, masks have been utilized in the theater to represent characters, animals, and ideas, and have often been used to commemorate important social customs and rituals.

There are mask variations that exist in cultures around the world. Here are some that are specific to different themes and traditions:

- Venetian Carnival masks

- Mexican Day of the Dead masks

- Chinese New Year masks

- Brazilian Carnival masks

- Filipino Dinagyang masks

- African Festima masks

- Bahamian Junkanoo masks

- Austrian Krampusnacht Festival masks

- Venezuelan Dancing Devils of Yare masks

- Japanese Shimokita Tengu Matsuri masks

- Japanese Noh drama masks

Artful use: Masks are frequently used in fine art, craft art, and outsider art, as a way to convey ideas about people and society. We see masks made as works of art in civilizations all over the world. Masks are a way of exploring a person's identity (Knight 2016; Wadeson 2000; Zwicky 2010), and lend themselves towards use in dramatic play, theatrical dynamics, and performance. Art therapists frequently use masks as a tool in helping people explore their inner self as well as the self that they promote and share with the world (Brumleve n.d.; Buchalter 2015; Corrington 2012; Dunn-Snow and Joy-Smellie 2011; Kaimal 2017; Makin 2000). Masks can be used as a tool in helping people to know themselves, since they are representational and often elicit some projection from the artist (Buchalter 2009).

Goals

- To experiment with taking on a different "persona" through the art of mask making.

- To encourage a deeper awareness of personal qualities or traits in an embodied character.

- To create a character around a trait or quality that the participant wishes they did or did not have.

- To create a character based on a part of the participant that is hidden and naturally unseen or intentionally "masked."

- To enhance the use of clear communication skills in the service of self-discovery.

Warm-ups

Masked name game

Using half-masks, distribute a mask to each group member. Invite them to put it on and prepare to become someone else. Inform participants that they have just arrived at a party where they are now invited by the hostess/host (i.e. the group facilitator) to introduce themselves to everyone. Participants can come up with a new name (real or imaginary). Let participants know that they can choose a new name, a new way to talk, stand, or move. If they are having difficulty coming up with an idea of who to be, encourage them to take inspiration from a character from a favorite book or TV show; perhaps there is someone they know that they've always wanted to be like, and now is a chance to try out that identity. Remind participants that there is no right or wrong in this exercise, and that using their imagination for exploration can be fun.

Self-mask

Have participants imagine that their face might freeze in a single pose or expression. Give a few minutes for trying out various "looks" or facial expressions and considering what these expressions might be called. They might be based on emotion, looks, or something else entirely (e.g. angry, slanted eyebrows, mad at the world, etc.). After everyone has had a chance to consider how their own face might be contorted, and what that contortion might represent or be called, encourage each participant to choose a single "frozen" facial expression or self-mask. Invite each participant to take a turn in showing their self-mask to the others, and sharing its title or description.

Venetian Carnival masks

Background

The Venetian *maschera* (Italian word for "mask") were first documented from the 13th century (Sethre 2003), although there is little known about why they came about. One theory suggests that Venetians responded to strict social class hierarchies by covering their faces in public (Johnson 2011). During the annual Carnival festival, laws that attempted regulation of consumption as a means of limiting luxury and decadence were suspended, which is why the Carnival has come to be associated with such extravagance. People used Carnival as a time to indulge in food, clothing, and luxury goods, and took advantage of this time as a break from strictly enforced social hierarchies (Burke 2005). The practice of wearing masks for disguise reached its height in the 18th century when Venetians of different social classes used masks as an excuse to mingle without fear of recognition or retribution. Wearing a mask—along with a silk hood, a cape, and a tricorn (a three-cornered hat)—people were tempted to behave in ways they wouldn't normally behave because their identity was hidden.

Masks served an important social purpose of keeping every citizen on an equal playing field. Masked servants could be mistaken for noblemen, state inquisitors and spies could question citizens without fear of their identity being discovered, and citizens could answer without fear of being punished.

As a result, people found themselves taking advantage of the situation. By the fall of the Venetian Republic, masks were banned and limited only to certain months of the year. This period extended for over three months starting on December 26th, and eventually shortened to week-long festivities that now comprise Carnival, elsewhere known as Mardi Gras.

Carnival, or *Carnevale*, takes place for eight days before Lent each winter. Tourists flood Venice for pageants, *Commedia dell'arte* ("comedy of professional artists" or "comedy of humors"), concerts, and masquerade balls until Shrove Tuesday (Fat Tuesday) signals an end to the party.

   Carnevale isn't just a Venetian tradition; similar festivities occur throughout much of the Roman Catholic world, including other cities in Italy. The term *carnevale* comes from the Latin for "farewell to meat," and suggests a goodbye party for the steaks and stews that Catholics traditionally gave up during the weeks of fasting before Easter. The masquerade aspect of *Carnevale* is even older: the Romans celebrated winter with a fertility festival where masks were worn by citizens and slaves alike.

Materials
Essentials

Mask forms with elastic (could be just eyes or whole face)

Tacky craft glue

Scissors

Decorative elements

Options and alternatives

Specialty papers

Tag board

Air-dry modeling clay (lightweight, such as Model Magic)

Felt

Chenille stems (pipe cleaners)

Hole punchers

Acrylic paints

Metallic paints

Bells

Ribbon/raffia

Sewing notions

Feathers

Glitter glue

Preparation

- Discuss the background information above in your own words, and share images of Venetian Carnival masks that you can find online. We recommend always showing multiple examples, since that helps participants to avoid the pitfall of mistakenly believing that there is one right way to create their own mask.

- Demonstrate combining different colors of modeling clay to create a marble effect. Or blend two colors to create a brand new color! Lightweight air-dry clay products are also easily painted or colored with markers.

Process

1. Encourage participants to think about a character they would like to be at the Carnival. They can use their imagination to be someone they have fantasized about being—maybe it's a favorite character from a book, movie, cartoon, etc. Remind participants that the beauty of a mask is that you can pretend to be someone other than yourself.

2. Using the materials available, each participant decorates a mask. If choosing to paint the mask, advise participants to use thin coats of paint to promote faster drying and to allow for other materials to be incorporated into the design. They can glue feathers, collage sheet music, or other specialty papers into the design.

3. Modeling clay can be used to "build up" specific areas such as creating a long nose like the *Nasone* Venetian masks or to build up the area at the top of the mask-making points, scallops, etc. Any area that has had modeling clay incorporated into it will be an easy place to stick feathers and other art materials.

4. Invite each person to "model" their mask in front of the other participants.

Questions for reflection or discussion

- Who is the character you have created? Have you given them a name?

- What did you discover about yourself through this mask-making process?

- What was the most fun about this project? What was the most difficult?

- Discuss what it was like to be someone else for a few moments—was it freeing? Inhibiting? Fun? Scary? Risky?

- What "masks" and "roles" do you play in real life?

- What associations and experiences do you have with masks?

The poem below is about the masks we wear, and encourages the reader to consider what we see when a mask is donned and what lies beneath. This might be a useful tool to prompt discussion about masks, or a creative writing activity that urges participants to consider their own use of masks, benefits, and liabilities to wearing masks, and how what we see on a mask may differ from what lies beneath.

We Wear the Mask (1896)
by Paul Laurence Dunbar (1872–1906)

We wear the mask that grins and lies,
It hides our cheeks and shades our eyes—
This debt we pay to human guile;
With torn and bleeding hearts we smile,
And mouth with myriad subtleties.
Why should the world be overwise,
In counting all our tears and sighs?
Nay, let them only see us, while
We wear the mask.

We smile, but, O great Christ,
our cries to Thee from tortured souls arise.
We sing, but oh the clay is vile
Beneath our feet, and long the mile;
But let the world dream otherwise,
We wear the mask!

Puerto Rican Vejigante masks

Background

The Vejigante is a Puerto Rican folkloric figure that makes frequent appearances in the processions of carnivals on the island. Their costumes include brightly colored horned masks and bat-like wings. There are two primary styles of masks, called *careta*, which are worn: those from the area of Loíza (Loíza Aldea Yearly Patron Saints Day n.d.), which are made from coconut husk, and those from the area of Ponce, which are papier-mâché. On the parade route they take on a trickster persona, carrying an inflated cow's bladder (*vejiga*) that they taunt, tease, and occasionally bop spectators with.

The most common theory regarding the origins of the Vejigante is based in the medieval Catholic legend of Saint James defeating the Moors (North African Islamic nomads), the Vejigantes representing the "infidel" Moors. As a character the Vejigante has been molded by a combination of cultural influences: Spanish, African, and native Taíno Indian. The resulting character is uniquely Puerto Rican.

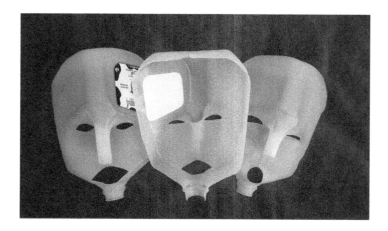

Materials
Essentials

Gallon milk/water jugs

Utility knife (for prepping jugs)

Copy paper*

Glue sticks

Masking tape

Decoupage medium*

Brushes

Paint

Scissors

Options and alternatives

Newspaper

50/50 mix of white glue and water as adhesive

* Copy paper and decoupage medium are recommended if a single session project because only a single layer is needed and the surface can be painted without full drying time. Alternatives are best used if the project is being made over multiple sessions.

Preparation

- Precut the milk or water jugs in half lengthwise. Flip them so that the handle appears to be a nose. Trim the handle/nose. Cut out eyes. Cut a mouth where the end of the handle was attached.

- Demonstrate how to make a paper cone for the horns. Cut a large semicircle from copy paper. Hold at the corners like a bib (flat side up), then gently bring the corners together, creating a cone. Tighten the cone to the desired width. Glue the leading edge closed. To secure the horns on to the jug, cut tabs at the base of the cone to increase the surface area, then use masking tape to secure them in place.

Process

1. Invite participants to make a simple sketch of their mask ideas on paper. Consider how many cones the mask will have. What colors will be used? How will they stylize it to make it their own?

2. Once they have a design plan, let participants choose a jug base for their mask—because they are hand cut, no two bases will be quite the same.

3. The next step is to make and attach paper cones. Review and demonstrate the process as needed. Some participants may find the idea of horns undesirable and use cones to create other featues such as sun-like rays, whiskers, or hats.

4. After the cones are in place, participants can then cover the mask. They should rip the copy paper into strips, then use a decoupage medium to adhere them to the surface of the jug. Using long strips at the base of the cones will help ensure that they are secure (Howcast 2009). Cones do not need to be covered with additional paper.

5. Participants can then paint their masks. If time constraints dictate, masks can be painted before they are fully dry.

Questions for reflection or discussion

- What kind of a persona does your mask embody? How is that demonstrated in your design?

- If you could design a costume to accompany your mask, what would it look like? Where might you wear it?

- How did your mask evolve from a sketch to the finished product? What influenced any changes?

Simple papier-mâché mask forms (with rice flour paste)

Background

The most basic thing needed for a mask project is the form. Pre-formed masks can be purchased, but can be cost-prohibitive. This is a simple recipe and technique for making forms yourself or with clients.

Materials

Aluminum foil

Newspaper strips

Rice flour paste:

½ cup rice flour

1 cup water

2 tbsp salt

Your choice of decorative materials

Process

- For the rice flour paste, the rice flour is mixed with the water and the salt and brought to a boil, stirred constantly for 3–5 minutes, until it reaches the desired consistency. The paste can be thinned with additional water.

- Participants create a mold with foil—they can form several layers to their own face, or just crumple and pinch it into the desired shape. They shouldn't worry about the details at this stage; this is just a base.

- Ask participants to dip strips of newspaper into the rice flour paste covering both sides, remove any excess, then add them to the foil face. They can pinch, fold, and add extra layers to accent eyes, nose, cheeks, etc. They should make sure to have at least three layers (remembering to alternate the direction of the strips).

- The masks can air dry or the process can be speeded up by setting the masks in an oven at around 250°F for 2–3 hours.

- The participants can decorate the masks with their choice of decorative materials.

3D construction paper masks

Background

Construction paper is one of the most common materials to have on hand, even on a sparse budget. Thankfully paper is such a versatile material! With just a few sheets, some scissors, and a glue stick, you have all you need for a mask. This pattern works well for inside/outside masks as both the convex and concave surface can be decorated.

Materials
Essentials

Construction paper	Scissors
Glue sticks	

Options and alternatives

Magazines	Collage material

Process

1. To create the base mask, have participants gently fold a sheet of construction paper vertically, avoiding creasing it. Then they should cut a large arc on the open side, creating an oval.

2. To give the mask a contour, participants should fold a 1"–2" triangle at the top and bottom of the oval, then reverse the fold of the triangle, creating a convex surface. They then glue the folded triangle secure to the inside. Eye holes can be cut at this time too (Cavendish 1975).

3. Paper scraps and strips can be used to decorate the mask. These can be shared scraps from other participants or additional materials provided.

4. Encourage participants to experiment with folding, twisting, and tearing paper to create contoured and textured facial features (Carlson 1994).

Chapter 2

Flags

Purpose

Flags have a deep significance to people in a variety of ways, making them ideal tools for the exploration of therapeutic goals. Flags are fabric signs, usually rectangular or triangular in shape, which have unique designs and meaningful colors on them. They are symbols that are banners of communication that connect people based on common experience or interests. People who are from the same state or country have the same flag. People who attended the same university are linked by a representative flag. Flags have been used throughout history in war, religion, education, maritime, and government. They are commonly associated with countries, but in the US states and cities also have their own flags. Organizations such as the United Nations and the International Olympic Committee have flags. While there are still circumstances where flags in practice are useful communication tools, such as in designating a safe swim area at the beach, or in indicating to race cars what lap they have achieved, in many places flags are ornamental "emblems of identity" (McCarthy 2010).

Flags allow people to adopt and express allegiance, self-concept, and connection. In this way they already function as markers of safe spaces and identity. Flags of a city or country, for example, might exemplify home, which for some people is a marker of safety. For other people, a flag is an emblem of safety in the form of asylum. Since people sometimes use flags as symbols of things that they feel connected to, such as their country, city, church, military, sports team, or cause, it is a natural extension that these flags might help define the person.

In art therapy flags are frequently developed as a symbol of the self (Buchalter 2009), or in the spirit of traditional Prayer Flags (Klammer n.d.; Miller 2011). Artists may be encouraged to choose colors, graphics, or symbols that represent themselves, or aspects of their real or aspirational identity.

Goals

- To identify qualities, values, or important aspects of self, and represent them with color, graphics, or symbols.

- To encourage a greater awareness of personal qualities or traits, as well as qualities that one is aspiring to.

- To exemplify primary values.

- To promote empathy, connection, community, and a sense of belonging.

Warm-ups

Whisper in the wind

Begin by explaining the premise of the game: the wind carries things from place to place. It transports many things like seeds and stray balloons across the skies. It can also help dissipate things like smoke and storm clouds. Tell participants that in this game you are going to utilize the wind's power to carry things, specifically, thoughts and intentions.

Invite participants to spend a moment thinking about the intention they would like to send. Depending on the participants and their personal goals you may want to suggest a theme such as "Worries you do not need" to ease stress, or "Something the world needs more of" to promote empathy.

Demonstrate how to make the sound of a soft wind by gently rubbing palms together. Softly blowing or a combination of both actions can also make this sound.

Once the sound of wind fills the space, participants then take turns whispering their thoughts into the wind. Encourage participants to open their hands to release, toss, or throw their thought, letting the wind carry it away. The game ends when everyone has had the opportunity to cast a thought or intention to the wind.

Fabric check-in

This warm-up activity helps to illustrate the connections and associations that are held by objects, specifically fabrics. That connection can be to a person, time, or place. This activity can also increase group cohesion and promote empathy as participants recognize parallels in their experiences.

In advance of the session ask participants to look for something made of fabric that they can bring with them to the group. The object could be a piece of clothing such as a special t-shirt, a practical object like a potholder, or something that has been handed down through the generations like a quilt or christening dress. You can also provide a selection of fabric scraps for participants to choose from in case anyone has forgotten to bring their own.

In the familiar format of "show-and-tell" participants take turns sharing the fabric item they have brought with them. Encourage the sharing of personal history or short anecdotes that each participant associates with the fabric. If participants are using a scrap you provided, ask them to share something that it reminds them of.

Some questions that can facilitate meaningful participation in this activity are: How does this object connect you to your history, family, or culture? When you recall a memory associated with the fabric, what other senses (smells, sounds, etc.) are initiated? Has the personal meaning of the item changed over time? If so, in what way?

Depending on time available and group members, it can be useful to offer some parameters around the sharing regarding length. This can be done by offering a specific guiding question at the beginning of the activity or establishing a defined duration such as a sentence count.

Tibetan Prayer Flags

Background

The making and hanging of Prayer Flags dates back thousands of years, both in India and in the pre-Buddhist Bon religious tradition of Tibet. The tradition has been continued through the centuries by Tibetan Buddhists and is still practiced today.

Prayer Flags (also called Dharma Banners) are said to contain well wishes and prayers, spreading peace, compassion, strength, and wisdom with the person who hangs them as well as people in the vicinity. They are hung such that the wind blows through the flags, so the blessings can be carried and shared wherever the wind touches (Radiant Heart Studios 2014).

The colors of traditional Prayer Flags represent the elements: blue symbolizes the sky and space, white symbolizes the air and wind, red symbolizes fire, green symbolizes water, and yellow symbolizes earth. Prayer Flags also feature animals and mantras (prayers) with significance within the Buddhist religion (Barker 2003; Beer 2004; The Rubin Museum of Art n.d.; Wise 2002).

Prayer Flags have an inherent communal intention. In recent history, the making and displaying of them has been embraced as an exercise of goodwill and healing by people of many faiths from around the world. There are tons of great ideas that you can see online for designing your own modern Prayer Flags (The Prayer Flag Project 2016). Prayer Flags can be a wonderful project for anyone considering a goal, a wish, a dream, an intention, or a hope, whether for oneself or the world. This project also lends itself towards consideration of the self in the community, since individuals can create their own flag representative of their own prayer or wish, and then connect it with the flags of others for a community display.

Materials
Essentials

Heavy cloth for background (approximately 9" x 12")

Yarn, cord, string, ribbon

Tacky glue

Large craft sticks or dowels

Materials for decorating

Options and alternatives

Assorted fabric scraps

Needles and thread

Buttons, beads, and notions

Chenille stems (pipe cleaners)

Permanent or fabric markers

Paper and pencils (for sketching ideas)

Preparation

- Precut the cloth background pieces.

- Demonstrate different ways to connect the materials (e.g. knotting, sewing, gluing, weaving, attaching with chenille stems, tying with string or twine, etc.).

Process

1. Ask participants to consider their intent (security, calm, good health, etc.). Remind them to be mindful and hold that intent in mind as they work on their flags.

2. Hand out the background cloth pieces and then ask participants to explore the materials offered, considering how the materials could support their design and intent.

3. Before laying out the design, participants should tuck the top 1"–1½" of the background under, reserving it for the hanging cord.

4. Participants then create a fabric collage using the materials offered, embellishing with buttons, beads, notions, and any other materials offered.

5. Once the design is finished, they can add the hanging cord by tucking a craft stick or dowel along with the cord into the fold at the back, and then glue or seal it closed.

6. The flags can then be hung together or individually.

Questions for reflection or discussion

- If you are working with a group, invite them to consider and discuss how working collaboratively influenced their design. What were some similarities that were identified? Differences?

- Where will you hang the flag(s)? Who do you hope the intent you had in mind reaches?

- Were you able to remain mindful throughout the art-making process? How did it feel to try to focus intent into an object you were making?

CULTURAL SIGNIFICANCE: AN EXAMPLE

In 2011, I was presenting as an invited guest speaker at a creative arts therapy conference in San Juan, Puerto Rico. I had the privilege of spending the day with a dynamic and creative group of professionals—some aspiring art therapists, and several in related mental health professions. Every part of my presentation exploring therapeutic goals and the accompanying art directives that I linked were met with curiosity, intrigue, and open-minded consideration.

Part way through the day, I brought up a flag project that I had developed and was excited to share. I had successfully used the project with many individual clients and groups and was confident that it inspired creativity. The project was to invite participants to create their own individual flags. The premise of the project was that just as state and national flags have colors, graphics, and symbols representing ideals and virtues, so, too, could individuals represent their values and identity on a flag. As I had done previously I planned to start off the directive with a discussion of flags, their meaning and purpose, and examine examples that we were all familiar with. I had boldly printed color copies of both the US flag and the flag of Puerto Rico. To my surprise, the introduction did not go at all like others had. As soon as I displayed the two flags, the group devolved into an intensely heated discussion about the past, present, and future of Puerto Rico. Simply by displaying the flags I had unintentionally initiated a discourse on a highly controversial topic.

I learned so much that day as my participants patiently explained to me the debate regarding the status of Puerto Rico in relation to the US. I learned of the three political action groups and their views on the future of Puerto Rico. Some participants wanted to see the island nation stand on its own; some wanted to see Puerto Rico achieve full statehood. Still others wanted Puerto Rico to remain a territory of the US with all of the existing privileges and challenges that are faced under the existing system. These two flags were a meaningful symbol to these participants, because they represented their homeland and the potential of what their island could be. In addition, there is a debate about the origin and designer of the Puerto Rican flag, and a complicated history, as "police used to arrest anyone displaying the flag on charges of insubordination against the United States" (The Flag of Puerto Rico n.d.).

In therapy and education we frequently reroute our plans in light of spontaneous developments. This was exactly that kind of group. Furthermore, individuals felt that their identity was tied up in limbo based on this ongoing debate about Puerto Rican statehood. It was hard for participants to access the idea of developing a personal flag when they had such complex relationships with the official flags of Puerto Rico and the US. In this way, I had to acknowledge that this directive, if pushed, could do more harm than good. Instead, I honored their desire to discuss the issues, and provided space for them to express their thoughts and frustrations.

My project from that day: Personal flags

- Materials: Paper, pencils, ruler, drawing supplies, fabric, acrylic paint, and paint brushes.

- Procedure: Discuss how flags may represent individuals who belong to a specific country, community, or culture, including special organizations, social, or spiritual groups. Invite participants to list the groups that they feel associated with, and any symbols associated with that particular group. Then invite participants to create a flag that includes colors, symbols, or graphics that represent aspects of themselves, significant events, or memories, and personal values.

- Goals: Increase self-awareness, enhance communication, promote intercultural tolerance, and increase self-esteem.

- Discussion: Focus on formulating a personal and community identity. What colors, shapes, or designs did you choose, and what do they symbolize or represent?

Mailable message streamers

Background

Flag projects can be done in a variety of sizes and with a number of different materials. This project is unique in that it can easily fold and fit into an envelope to be sent in the mail or included in an altered book or journal.

Materials

Crepe paper party streamer

Copy paper

String

Crayons or markers

Reinforcement labels (stickers that reinforce pages in ring binders) or masking tape

Scissors

Hole punch

Preparation

- If you are working in a setting with materials restrictions such as no sharps, precut 24" lengths of streamer and paper shapes (hearts, word or thought bubbles, diamonds, etc.).

Process

1. Ask participants to consider what message they would like to share, such as things they are thankful for, personal strengths and attributes, or an inspirational quote.

2. Participants can then cut out shapes from paper to write their message on (if not already precut). Shapes should be about 2"–3".

3. Using crayons or markers they can write their messages, and make them as fancy or as plain as they like.

4. Message shapes are then glued down the length of the streamer, leaving about 2" at the top for hanging.

5. In order to prevent the streamer from ripping, participants should place a reinforcement label or a small tab of masking tape at the top, then punch a hole through it and add a string for hanging.

Paper pennant flags

Background

Pennant flags are triangle-shaped flags that can be seen hanging as long banners in front of newly opened stores, or waved overhead at college sporting events, for example. Because of their related context, many people associate them with applause, congratulation, and accomplishment.

While these blank flags can be used as a base for many directives, we feel that they are especially well suited for addressing self-esteem. Participants can create a pennant to celebrate an accomplishment or attribute that they are proud of or a banner of them representing multiple aspects of themself. Couples and families can make banners together, celebrating each other.

Materials
Essentials

Copy paper

Ruler

Scissors

Straws/chopstick/dowel (handle for a single flag)

or

String/ribbon/yarn (to hang multiple flags)

Options and alternatives

Crayons, markers, colored pencils

Collage materials

Preparation

- Mark and cut out the banner pieces. On one 11" side of the paper measure 5½" and on the other measure 2¼" in from each edge. Make a line from the corner to the 2¼" mark, then back up to the 5½" mark, down to the other 2¼" then back to the top corner. This will give you three banners or flags (and two smaller triangle scraps) per sheet.

Process

1. Show participants how to fold the wide end of their pennant down about ¾" and trim the corners flush with the banner edge, reserving it for the string or straw.

2. Invite participants to decorate the flags in a way that is meaningful to them using drawing or collage materials. When designing, they should keep in mind that a single flag will be held horizontal while banners hang vertical.

3. Once they are decorated, participants can prepare their flags for waving. For a single flag, tuck the handle into the ¾" fold and glue into place. For a banner fold the edge over the string and glue closed (Youngs 2010).

Super simple bunting banners

Background

These bunting banners feature semicircle-shaped flags that can be customized. They are simple and require few materials, making them appropriate for almost any setting.

Materials

Round coffee filters*   Glue sticks

String, yarn, or ribbon   Markers or crayons

*   Use restaurant coffee urn filters for an oversized banner.

Preparation

- String can be cut in advance, eliminating the need for scissors if in a no sharps setting.

Process

1. Demonstrate how to fold the coffee filter in half over the string, which is then closed with glue.

2. Invite participants to decorate with a theme and materials of their choice.

3. The banners can be dressed up by adding pieces of crepe paper streamer glued the same way.

Chapter 3

Boxes

Purpose

Boxes make wonderful art materials and bases for an array of art projects. Boxes come in all different shapes, sizes, and materials. They are frequently free. They can sometimes be stored flat or stacked inside of other boxes, taking up very little precious art supply storage space. They have all sorts of qualities that parallel natural metaphors that we use for personal qualities and interpersonal interactions: boxes can be open or closed, they can contain within or create a boundary to keep out, they can conceal or be visible, they can be sturdy or lack structural integrity. Boxes facilitate exploration of the dichotomy of the self in relation to the other: inside and outside, top and bottom, closed and open.

Box projects are commonly used in art therapy. The box often serves as a canvas on which to project a representation of the self (Farrell-Kirk 2001; Kaufman 1996; Landgarten 1981; Liebmann 1986; Pifalo 2007; Waller 2014). Professionals have written about the use of boxes as a tool for self-care tips, coping skills, or reminders, or as containers for memories, dreams, or ideas (Hrenko 2005; Moon 2011; Morgan 2001). Boxes could contain issues, stressors, problems, or past trauma (Chu 2010; Rappaport 2009). They may be used to facilitate a single purpose, as with scream boxes or safe boxes. In some art therapy scenarios, clients are invited to build a safe space, conceived of through art materials (Leasure 2017). Boxes that are fragile or delicate, especially when small, connote a value and importance, as with jewelry boxes.

We ascribe great value to things that need a container to protect them. What sort of box projects can you conceive of?

Goals

- To create a tangible safe space through art that can serve as a container for memories, ideas, stress, precious things, or the exploration of self.

- To encourage an awareness of personal qualities projected on to or reflected by the box, such as openness, accessibility, boundaried, or enclosed.

- To create a piece of art that has utility and function (e.g. coping box, memory box, or scream box).

- To provide an opportunity for a participant to recognize, establish, and maintain or modify personal boundaries.

Warm-ups

Can you see what I see?

This activity is a fun way to illustrate the importance and challenges of accurate communication. It can be played with couples, several pairs of people, or with one person being the viewer and multiple people drawing.

You will need paper, pencil, a box for each pair of participants, and some everyday objects that will fit inside. The participants should not see the objects in advance.

Explain that in this game one participant is the viewer and the other(s) will draw. The problem is that only the viewer can look inside the box at the object. That person must describe what they see in terms of size, texture, shape, etc., and without naming or directly describing the object, for example, "It is one of the four rubber pieces under a car that roll"—the other participant(s) must draw the object from only that description.

Ask participants to choose who will view and who will draw. Seat them in such a way that only the viewer can see inside the box (across a table or back to back). Start the game! When 2–3 minutes has passed ask participants to stop. They should then share what they have created, first with each other, and then with the group (Anderson 2010).

Spend a few minutes reflecting on the activity. Ask participants to consider what emotions they noticed as they participated. Did it change as time passed? What was it like to depend on another person so completely for something they are accustomed to doing themselves? How do they think it would be different if they changed roles?

What is it?

This warm-up is designed to encourage brainstorming skills, open-mindedness, and imaginative play.

Put a box (any size, any shape) in the middle of the table and ask participants to brainstorm a list of all of the things it could be, do, or be used for. They may come up with some obvious responses, such as, "it could hold things" or "wrap a present," as well as more creative or silly ideas, like, "it could shovel snow," "be recycled," or "toy storage." Encourage participants to think broadly, to push the limits of their imagination, and not to self-edit.

Participants can work individually, in small groups, or all together as a larger team. Give a certain amount of time for the activity, and after calling time and counting responses, ask participants to see if they can come up with just two or three more ideas.

Spend a few minutes reflecting on the activity. Some questions you can use to prompt discussion could be: What was your first idea? Best idea? Most conventional idea? Most bizarre idea? Was your imagination sparked in any way by the responses or ideas of others? In what other areas of life do we brainstorm in this way, or where might this sort of brainstorm activity be useful?

Pieces of me—Monochromatic assemblage boxes

Background

Assemblage is the sculptural counterpart to collage: a three-dimensional composition made from a variety of traditionally nonartistic materials and objects. The materials for assemblage can come from almost anywhere and consist of almost anything. Found objects such as bottle caps, shells, foam letters, clothespins, random puzzle pieces, wood scraps, keys, and small toys are all art materials!

This project is specifically inspired by the works of the American sculptor Louise Nevelson (1899–1988), a pioneer in the art of assemblage: "She constructed abstract compositions by arranging scavenged bits of discarded wood in boxes, stacking them to form sculptural walls and environments, and unifying them by painting them a single color" (National Museum of Women in the Arts n.d., para. 4). Other artists whose work in assemblage might be used as inspiration for this or other projects include Judith Scott (Creative Growth n.d.), Joseph Cornell, Isa Genzken, Robert Rauschenberg, and Betye Saar (Kordic 2016).

SIMILAR AND DIFFERENT

The ability to identify likeness and difference is part of the human condition. In fact, comparing and contrasting is part of how we make sense of our world in every forum of life. In art and writing we sometimes look for distinctions and commonalities, and sometimes we even create them as a means of expressing a point.

Using the intention of likeness as a unifying factor can help forge connections, bonding, and dispose of the "otherness" that is so prevalent in much of the world and in people's experiences. People, it turns out, are seeking connection.

Consider bringing the discussion of similarities and differences intentionally into your therapy group or classroom. Charge your participants with identifying likenesses in words, experiences, art, form, or function. And consider inviting your participants to work towards finding a connection by telling them that there needs to be a unifying quality. I might instruct a group of participants to make sure that their art pieces share a common design element, which could be a color, shape, size, material, or other style choice. This group decision-making opportunity challenges participants to communicate, collaborate, and negotiate, even if they get to make their own art. It challenges them to create in a way that requires some discussion, and perhaps some compromise. In this way, working together on a common goal, even if contrived, can facilitate the building of relationships and interpersonal skills.

Materials
Essentials

Small box

Glue gun*

Toothpicks

Single-color acrylic paint

Paint brush

Assorted assemblage materials such as buttons, beads, silk flowers, tiny toys, keys, puzzle pieces, Lego, foam stickers, bottle caps, etc.... Be imaginative with the objects you bring!

Options and alternatives

Air-dry clay

---

* As an alternative to using hot glue, the box base can be filled with air-dry clay and objects pressed into it. If objects become dislodged after the clay dries, glue them into place with tacky glue.

Process

1. Ask participants to spend some time considering the variety of objects offered for this activity. Suggest that they take notice of any specific materials they are drawn to, noting the shape, size, and texture. Remind them that the color, including any printing, will not be relevant to the final piece.

2. Have them choose materials for their assemblage and the box they will use. They can then plan their composition, including what might go on the inside or outside of the box. Remind them that sometimes we have seemingly contradictory thoughts, feelings, or traits, and ask how they might represent this within their piece.

3. If necessary, demonstrate how to use a hot glue gun to assemble the piece. A toothpick can be used to aid in situating pieces in tight spaces and to keep fingertips safe.

4. After all the pieces are secured, invite participants to select what color they will paint their assemblage. Is there a color that holds special significance? The color will become the attribute that all pieces of the assemblage will have in common.

5. Participants should paint their entire assemblage box. It may require a second coat if original colors of objects show through after the paint dries.

Questions for reflection or discussion

- What are some of the found objects that you chose to include? Did any of them carry associations for you? In what way?

- How did your assemblage change when you painted it? Did you have an emotional reaction to that change?

- Are there any objects that you obscured from view or are hidden within your assemblage box? If so, what was your intent in doing so?

Russian lacquer decorative boxes

Background

Lacquer box making is a traditional art that has been practiced for centuries in Russia. These boxes contain brightly colored miniature paintings and are so polished that they seem to glow. They often depict fairy tales, battle scenes, or landscapes, and are edged with a decorative border of gold. As with many traditional arts, distinctive variations in style and themes exist dependent on the area where they are made. Artists sign works not only with their name, but also with their village and the year the works were made, connecting the art and artist to a time and place (Reyes Berry 1982; Stonebarger n.d.).

Materials
Essentials

Small- to medium-sized box (this can vary depending on purpose and availability)

Decoupage medium

Assorted collage materials such as magazines, photos, decorative paper, tissue paper

Scissors

Wide brush (½" works well for applying decoupage medium)

Options and alternatives
These materials can be used/added after the surface has dried:

Permanent markers or paint pens

Buttons, gems, sequins

Ribbon, yarn, cord

Tacky glue or glue gun

Preparation

- Remove any packets of silica gel or other waste often found in repurposed and new boxes.

- Precut images and words help to alleviate the distraction that full magazines sometimes present.

- If participants are unfamiliar with decoupage medium, prepare a surface for demonstration. Be sure to note that a thick coat of decoupage medium will result in a tacky surface and should be avoided, and that it works best to adhere modest-sized pieces, not full sheets.

Process

1. Ask participants to consider the purpose that their box will serve. Will it represent them inside and out? Will it serve as a container for a Crisis Survival Kit (a personalized collection of tools used to increase distress tolerance)? What kinds of images, words, or simply colors can embody their intent?

2. Have participants choose and collect the materials they would like to use on their box. If covering a repurposed box, tissue paper can be used to create a solid background for other images.

3. Using decoupage medium, have participants decorate their box with their chosen materials. Decoupage medium acts as both an adhesive and a sealant, so will be applied under and over as so: using a paint brush, lightly coat a small area of the box with decoupage medium, lay the image on the space, then brush a layer over it, sealing it into place. This top layer gives the boxes a lacquered shine.

4. After the box has fully dried, decorative accents from the optional and alternative materials list can be added.

Questions for reflection or discussion

- How did you organize your composition? Are there some images that cover others? Inside and outside? How did you choose what would go where?

- A box is a practical object. How did the utilitarian nature of the object impact your art making?

- Did personalizing the box make it feel any more or less useful to you? In what way?

- Is there any specific element that you included that reflects your culture or background or experience? Did you include anything that connects it to this time and place?

Doors

Background

Doors are a potent symbol. They can represent a barrier, a threshold, a boundary, or the potential for movement into a changed environment (Squire 1996). A door can signify choice or it can offer a sense of security. Similar to boxes, they are a visual representation of containment, and can also serve as metaphors for openness in places, people, and relationships (MacKenzie 2015). "Doors are often utilized in our vernacular to represent opportunity," wrote Crenshaw and Green (2009, p.7). "A job well-done may open doors for advancement while closed doors may represent self-sabotage and underachievement, or lack of ambition. A door partly open may suggest new possibilities or potentials. Doors open or closed or part-way open may symbolize key relationships in the child's life. Closed doors may represent rejection, deprivation, or missing out while open doors the opposite" (Crenshaw and Green 2009, p.7). In this way, doors can make wonderful metaphors that can represent other things going on in life.

A contemporary illustration of this symbolism is represented by the folklore of fairy doors. These miniature doors are thought of as portals between the fairy world and our own. The owner of the door needs only to believe in the magic for it to work (Boyd 2016).

Some artists believe that working with natural materials such as sticks, shells, or stones is a process of bringing out the art inherently contained within them. As such they may choose to minimize alterations and enhance features such as textures or crevices (Abrams 1990; Art Story Contributors 2018; Goldsworthy 2015; Mok 2009; Nicolas 2015; Zella 2017).

Materials
Essentials

Sticks, 5"–10" and about finger-width work well

Chenille stems (pipe cleaners)

Natural embellishments (feathers, shells, dried flowers, grasses, pine cones, etc.)

Options and alternatives

String, yarn, ribbon

Buttons, beads, notions

Scissors

Preparation

- Collect suitable-sized sticks in advance.

- If necessary, cut string, yarn, or ribbon. This eliminates the need for scissors, making the project suitable for facilities with materials restrictions (i.e. no sharps).

Process

1. Invite participants to consider what their door will represent. Are they fortifying a boundary? Inviting potential? Ask them to keep this intent in mind as they choose materials.

2. Participants should choose 4–6 sticks and 2 chenille stems. Demonstrate how to assemble the door. Bend the chenille stem (pipe cleaner) in half, forming a "V." Lay your first stick in the crook of the "V" then twist it closed (imagine closing a bread bag). Repeat with the other chenille stems. Lay the next stick into the newly formed "V"s, lancing the two sticks

together side by side. Repeat with more sticks until the door is the desired width.

3. Participants can then decorate their doors using natural embellishments, such as ribbon or string, and additional chenille stems can also be used to secure adornments.

Questions for reflection or discussion

- Does your door have a handle? A window? A knocker or bell? Why, or why not?

- How is your intent illustrated in your door? How did your intent evolve as you worked? What prompted that change (if there was one)?

- How did the materials impact your process? How do you think it would differ if you were working with finished dowels or craft sticks?

- If you could install your door anywhere, where would that be? How long would it remain there?

LIFE RAFTS: A METAPHOR

At a certain point in the process of creating your door, you will have a group of small sticks arranged and bound by chenille stems, and this may resemble a small and rustic river raft, or a floating life raft. Drop it in the bathtub and you may see that it does, in fact, float. You might even decide that you like this piece that functions as and represents a life raft. In actuality, there is much use for metaphoric life rafts in therapy, and in discussion and development of life resources, coping skills, and useful defense mechanisms.

Frank (2017, para. 1) writes, "For clients, being in the midst of chaos feels like being in the middle of the ocean with no vessel, flailing arms in hopes that someone might see and help." We can only assess the value of our life rafts after learning the intensity of the water conditions, the size of the waves, the depth of the water, the speed of the current, and how harsh the environment might be. Goldberg and Stephenson (2016) write about the value of working within metaphor in therapy. Art that visually invites a metaphor makes this process easier.

Using life rafts as a figurative tool in therapy can be useful and productive. Reiter (2017, p.236) demonstrates responding with questions about a metaphoric life raft to a client who expresses feelings of "sinking." In some cases, life rafts might even be literal tools, or symbolic tools created in art. Certainly there is much to be extracted from the symbolism of having a tool that can actually save a life. This might provide a topic that is rich for discussion in any therapeutic or educational space.

Faux-stained glass windows

This project is a great example of something that could be changed in a variety of ways to fit your space, audience, and materials. We urge you to reference Appendix 2: *Customization Considerations*, and to think of other adaptations that you might make.

Faux-stained glass windows offer a wide variety of tactile materials without the need for sharps or wet adhesives. The project is exceptionally well suited for young children or special needs clients. At the same time, older clients or those with more art experience can also enjoy it while making more sophisticated designs. Introducing unique parameters that fit your group theme or limiting materials are some ways to evolve this project. Window frames can be designed in a variety of shapes or around educational, holiday, seasonal, religious, or therapeutic themes. The variations on a given project are endless.

Background

Like boxes and doors, windows are a potent symbol of containment. Among other things, they can represent a barrier and distance or an area of introspection and understanding. Stained or colored glass is often associated with spirituality and places of worship. By changing the lighting of an area, it can provide an otherworldly feel, enhancing a sense of safety or containment.

There is evidence of stained glass windows in churches and monasteries in Britain as early as the 7th century. By the Middle Ages stained glass had become a major art form in much of Western Europe. These windows were mostly found in churches and mosques, the institutions of higher learning at that time. Pictures depicted in the art served as illustrations of texts and were a tool for teaching a largely illiterate population.

The glass used in stained glass windows was originally colored by adding different elements such as cobalt, nickel, or copper. Strips of lead were used between the pieces of glass to hold them together. This is why the lines in a stained glass window are called "leading" (Hayward n.d.; Southwick 2011).[1]

Materials
Essentials

Contact paper or self-adhesive laminate sheets

Colored duct tape or wide masking tape

Assorted scraps of tissue paper, yarn, feathers, sequins, small pom-poms, fortune cookie papers, etc.

Options and alternatives

Transparency paper

Black construction paper (optional)

Preparation

- Cut contact paper to the desired working size (usually 9" x 12").

- Peel the backing at all four corners and then tack the sheet to the workspace with masking tape. This will prevent the sheet from curling or pulling up while the participants work.

- Precut black construction paper into ½" strips, if using in a restricted materials environment.

---

1   http://stainedglass.org

Process

1. Ask participants to consider the purpose they would like their window to serve. Is it to keep things out or to let things in? Will it include an illustration or words? Will it have panes or leading to define a design?

2. When participants are ready to begin, peel the backing from the contact sheet revealing the adhesive surface. Using the materials offered they can create a design. Objects such as pom-poms, yarn, and sequins can be repositioned. Black paper strips can be used to define panes or leading.

3. Once the design is finished, participants can set a translucent sheet (or second piece of laminate) atop, then press together allowing any uncovered adhesive to attach the surfaces closed, and trim the sheet as needed.

4. Participants can then edge the entire design with tape by applying a strip of tape along one side as if securing the window to the table, then flipping it over and folding the unsecured tape onto the other side. They should repeat this on all sides. This will both create a frame and further secure the contents of the design.

Questions for reflection or discussion

- How is your purpose reflected in your design? How did it impact the materials you chose?

- How did it feel when you first held your design up and looked through it? Was there anything in particular you noticed?

- If you could install your window anywhere, where would that be? What impact do you hope it would have on that space?

Chapter 4

Charms, Talismans, Amulets

Purpose

Across cultures and throughout time people have long ascribed value to a variety of charms, talismans, amulets, and symbols that can be similarly characterized. In some cases these tools and objects, frequently associated with a specific religious tradition or cultural group, are believed to bring good luck, to ward off evil, or to provide spiritual protection. Amulets are typically associated with things that are worn on a person, and some are believed to have magic powers. Examples of these auspicious objects include horseshoes, a rabbit's foot, pendants, coins, scrolls, mezuzahs, dream catchers, a crucifix, tefillin, four-leafed clover, milagros, nazar, and the sacred heart. Not all of these objects carry the same weight and significance, but to different people and communities, different objects are important, or even sacred. This subject is discussed further at the beginning of Section 1, "Appreciation vs. appropriation: Note of intention."

Goals

- To encourage the use of imagination and the creative process.

- To provide the opportunity for participants/artists to create symbols of protection and good fortune.

- To promote a sense of wellbeing.

- To provide participants with the opportunity to creatively embody tools for mindfulness and distress tolerance.

- To encourage participants to consider issues of luck, fate, and locus of control.

- To introduce concepts of ritual and objects of hope.

Warm-ups
Pack rats and neat freaks (Keepers and clearers)

In reality it doesn't matter if you are a self-proclaimed keeper of things or someone who cannot stand clutter—everyone has something that they hold on to. In this warm-up participants are invited to self-identify and explore an exaggerated stereotype of either a keeper or a clearer, and then interact in a way that provides the opportunity to disarm those stereotypes. This activity promotes dialectic thinking, empathy, and understanding by illustrating commonalities between opposing stereotypes.

Introduce the game by asking people to share if they consider themselves to be more of a keeper of things or clearer of spaces. Depending on your group, participants may connect these identifiers to a spectrum of behaviors, labels, or diagnosis such as collectors, pack rats, and hoarders or detail-oriented, neat freaks, and obsessive-compulsives.

Invite them to physically separate into groups based on this difference. After they have moved, in your own words emphasize the divide by theatrically introducing the groups to one another, stressing the differences between keepers and clearers.

Following the dramatic preface, instruct participants to mingle, sharing with each other *the one thing that they will never get rid of.* If possible, allow enough time for everyone to meet and share (The Able Trust 2009).

Spend a few minutes reflecting on the activity. Ask the participants: How did it feel to have the persona you chose emphasized and exaggerated into a stereotype? What impact did it have on your expectations about others in the group? How might your experience have been different if the commonality was emphasized instead of the differences? Did you find that you had anything in common with someone you didn't anticipate? In what areas of your life have you observed preconceptions affecting the way people interact?

Fortunately/unfortunately

This activity illustrates the black-and-white thinking that can sometimes impede our ability to effectively traverse a situation or relationship. By introducing it in the context of a game, the all-or-nothing rationale can be explored in a playful context.

Begin by explaining to participants that this game will require them to take the opposite view of whatever was just said. Explain that in order to do this they will listen to the statement of the person before them, and then preface their response with either "Fortunately" or "Unfortunately" (Anderson 2010).

Start play by sharing an event with a positive connotation. In groups where trust has not yet been established or an undercurrent of tension exists, a fanciful scenario can aid in keeping gameplay lighthearted.

For example, you might begin with, "Fortunately, I just got a magic wand for my birthday!" The next person would then respond with a negative aspect of that event, such as "Unfortunately, I have no idea how to use it." The next person's response should reflect a positive, "Fortunately, it came with instructions." "Unfortunately, my dog ate them." And so on.

Play continues until there is a natural conclusion or a designated time period ends it. The length of the game varies greatly depending on the size of the group.

If there is an even number of players, plan to play at least two rounds so that all participants have the opportunity to think of both fortunate and unfortunate responses.

Spend a few minutes reflecting on the activity. Ask participants: Was it fun, challenging, or frustrating? Was it easier to think of fortunate or unfortunate responses? Why do you think that was? Have you ever experienced this kind of extreme thinking in a real situation? How did it impact your effectiveness in that situation?

Khamsas (also written as Hamsas)

Background

** *Khamsa*, pronounced like hom-sa **

In many cultures, hands have always been symbols of strength, power, and protection. *Khamsas* are amulets, or good luck charms, in the form of a hand. They originated in Morocco, Africa and spread among many Mediterranean cultures.

The word *khamsa* means "five" and refers to the five fingers. Tradition has it that a *khamsa* with spread fingers wards off bad luck, while a closed-fingered hand brings good luck. The *khamsa* appears both in a two-thumbed, bilaterally symmetrical form and in a more natural form in which there is only one thumb. An alternative Islamic name for this charm is the *Hand of Fatima*, in reference to the daughter of Mohammed. An alternative Jewish name for it is the *Hand of Miriam*, in reference to the sister of Moses and Aaron.

Some *khamsas* are worn as pendants and are frequently made out of precious metals such as silver. Others are designed to hang near a doorway to protect the home and its occupants. No matter what their intent, the *khamsa* hand is positioned with fingers pointing downwards. Some have good luck animals, such as salamanders, incorporated into their designs. Others have precious stones and gems set into the metal (Gomez 1992; Yronwode n.d.).

Materials
Essentials

Heavy-duty aluminum foil	Scissors
Tag board	Hole punch
Ribbon/string/yarn	Glue sticks

Options and alternatives

Glass gems, buttons, beads, sequins

Wood stylus (for etching)

Specialty papers

Craft glue

Preparation

- Familiarize yourself with the history and cultural significance of *khamsas* so that you can explain them to participants in your own words.

- Precut the tag board to approximately 5" x 8".

Process

1. Begin by sharing the background of the *khamsa* as well as other symbols of luck and good fortune from around the world, such as the scarab in Egypt and the elephant with its trunk in the air in India and Asia. Invite participants to identify other examples of good luck symbols that they are familiar with from their own culture.

2. Demonstrate how to cover the tag board with foil. Tear off a piece of aluminum foil wide enough to cover the tag board front and back. Fold the foil in half and place a piece of the precut tag board between the foil. Using a glue stick, glue the foil to the tag board, smoothing out any creases.

3. Have participants place one hand on the aluminum foil form. Remind them of the different significance of hand positions: spread fingers ward off bad luck while a closed-fingered hand brings good luck. They should trace around the hand, fingers, and a bit of the wrist.

4. Next ask the participants to cut a hand shape out of the foil form. This can take some effort due to the thickness of the tag board and foil together. Encourage patience.

5. The participants then emboss their designs into their *khamsa* using the wooden stylus like a doodle design. Both sides of the hand can be decorated. Additional embellishments can be added by gluing on sequins, gemstones, and small shapes cut from specialty papers.

6. When the *khamsa* is finished, a hole can be punched in the area of the wrist so it can be hung upside down for good luck. String ribbon or yarn through the hole for hanging. Traditionally, *khamsas* hang near a doorway to promote good fortune!

7. Invite participants to share their *khamsa* with the group.

Questions for reflection or discussion

- What is special or significant about your *khamsa*? What does it symbolize to you?

- What will you do with your *khamsa*? Do you have a special place in mind to install it?

- How did you find the experience of working with these art materials? How did you work through any challenges as you went along?

Worry dolls

Background

The idea of a talisman having the power to take worries away is popular because worry is a universal experience. Worry dolls or *muñecas quitapenas* originated with indigenous people from the highlands of Guatemala. They are marketed with instructions to tell the doll your worries then sleep with it under your pillow, and the doll will magically carry your worries away (Ferguson n.d.; Port 2014). The dolls have long been popular souvenirs for tourists because of their size and relatively low cost.

Materials
Essentials

Bamboo cocktail forks	Scissors
Tacky glue	Fabric scraps

Options and alternatives

String, thread, ribbon	Tooth picks
Chenille stems (pipe cleaners)	Feathers

Preparation

- Gather materials to demonstrate different ways to make the arms.

- Depending on the practical skill level of the participants, you may also want to demonstrate knots and twists.

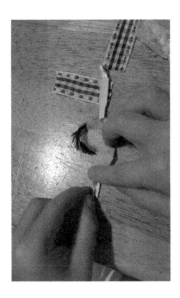

Process

1. Invite participants to consider what key characteristics they want their character to have. If they are making a set of dolls, will each doll carry away a different type of worry? What will the dolls have in common?

2. The participants then choose their materials, deciding what they will use for arms, clothing, hair, etc.

3. Share these helpful hints for "working small":

   - Use a toothpick to apply glue in small amounts to targeted spots.

   - Keep string long for tying, and trim after it is secured.

   - Cloth and string cut best when held taut—lend a hand.

4. Demonstrate how to secure the arms. If you are using chenille stems (pipe cleaners), these are wrapped securely around the body. Ribbon or yarn is knotted around the body. Toothpicks can be glued and then crisscross-tied with thread.

5. Participants can then dress the dolls up. We suggest:

   – Shirts and dresses can be added by making a tiny cut in the middle and sliding the fabric over the head.

   – String can be wrapped around any part to make pants, shirts, skirts, etc. Add a small amount of glue underneath to secure in place.

   – Hair can be glued on. Try a feather, some yarn, or a bit of frayed fabric.

6. Encourage participants to share their project. A fun way to do this is like an "I-Spy…" game, encouraging participants to seek commonalities while emphasizing the universal nature of worries and other emotions.

Questions for reflection or discussion

- Did you have a particular worry in mind as you worked? Did the intensity dissipate or change as you worked?

- How did working on a small scale impact your process?

- Will you keep the dolls for yourself or give them to other people? If you are planning to give them away, did you have that person in mind when you made it? Did you include anything special for them?

CULTURAL CONNECTIONS: WORKING WITH PEOPLE OF DIVERSE CULTURES

In many respects we want to approach our clients and students as people first and foremost, but we cannot forget the culture and heritage they bring into the room. The underpinnings of these cultures and experiences that they have had in spite of or because of their culture may explain a little about the issues they face, the changes or growth that they seek, and the manner in which they present in therapy, in education, and in life.

Our best shot at helping people happens when we work in a culturally sensitive manner (Potash *et al.* 2015). Cultural competence is a dynamic, not static, representation of a professional's ability to engage in therapeutic relationship, activities, viewpoints, and policies that allow them to function capably in cross-cultural situations. This means considering personal perspectives and biases, cultural norms of one's clinical training and orientation, and also understanding the obstacles and the importance of providing therapeutic services to a culturally diverse client base (Jackson, Mezzera and Satterberg 2017).

As an example, when working with Latinas, or women in the US of Latin or Hispanic descent, cultural awareness means acknowledging higher than typical incidences of traumatic experiences, socioeconomic challenges, and concerns pertaining to acculturation and deportation, as well as obstacles to mental health services and an underutilization of therapeutic services (Ciornai and Ruiz 2016; Jackson *et al.* 2017; Kouyoumdjian, Zamboanga and Hansen 2003).

Art therapy may be a useful tool and a natural fit for people who hail from cultures that are dynamically entrenched in art, as are many Latin cultures. The Mexican Day of the Dead festival (*El Dia de los Muertos*) is one of the clearest examples of art as a ritual tool in helping to process transition and loss (Linesch, Metzel and Trevino 2016). It incorporates art in a multitude of ways, from *ofrendas* and marigold garlands, to sugar skulls, milagros, lanterns, and flags. People celebrating *El Dia de los Muertos* embrace the celebration of life as well as the opportunity to honor, remember, and revere the dead. Guatemalan worry dolls have a rich tradition whereby people use small personified inanimate objects as tools for dealing with the uncertainty of life (Brown 2007; Ferguson n.d.; Kennedy 2015; Port 2014):

> Traditional forms of art making can provide Latinas with a platform for actively authoring their dreams, desires, hopes, and realities, while validating their traditional values and acknowledging the richness and the healing available through their cultural heritage. Culturally competent approaches to treatment incorporate a posture of cultural humility, in which a therapist remains interested, curious, open to, and welcoming of clients in ways that both enrich the relationship and welcome their clients' cultural values, principles, and beliefs. (Jackson *et al.* 2017)

Art therapy may also be a great fit for people with significant stressors and trauma history, and those wrestling with the identity formation issues that frequently accompany immigration or relocation. Activities that encourage personal and familial exploration can help address issues of identity that pertain to heritage and cultural pride.

Arpilleras, or story cloths, that hold memories and frequently trauma, helped to build the platform for the human rights movement in Chile (Strauss 2015). *Arpilleras* are a form of textile collage that frequently include weaving, sewing, and embroidery on a tapestry (Comas-Díaz and Jansen 1995) and are found in many Latin American traditions (Charland 2011). These frequently record personal and community trauma, including violence against women, protest against political regimes, and acts of war (Agosin 1996, 2014; Cohen 2013; Fry 1990; Moya-Raggio 1984; Reynolds 2000, 2004). Women who create *arpilleras* are called *arpilleristas*, and they frequently use the textile collage as a tool to help them contain, express, and placate their feelings of grief (Strauss 2015).

It is important to understand and consider the values and dominant cultural influences of the individuals you are working with. For example, individuals who are raised in cultures abundant with creative forms of self-expression, transitional rituals, and artful processing of trauma may be better prepared in creative ways when processing other events in their lives. Understanding the way cultural elements inform and help develop a person's self-conception and self-esteem will ultimately render therapeutic intervention more effective.

A mummy for this life

Background

Egyptian mummies were laid to rest with all of the things that they believed would be needed in the afterlife. For this project we borrow that idea, but with a twist, creating a talisman containing a gift for someone in this life. In doing this we guide participants in identifying intangible assets that improve quality of life and cultivate empathy and gratitude.

Materials
Essentials

Craft sticks	Tissue paper
Pen or pencil	Materials for wrapping and embellishing
Scissors	

Options and alternatives

String, yarn, ribbon, chenille stems (pipe cleaners), etc. for wrapping

Feathers, bells, beads, dried flowers, etc. for embellishing

Preparation

- If you are working with young participants or in a facility with materials restrictions (i.e. no sharps), eliminate the need for scissors by precutting 6" x 6" tissue paper squares (one each) and an assortment of wrapping materials to manageable lengths (about 12").

Process

1. Ask participants to consider whom their mummy will be for and what they feel that person needs. Suggest some things that people could often use more of in their lives: joy, laughter, confidence, luck, love, etc.

2. Instruct them to write a word or short phrase on a craft stick. This does not need to be shared with anyone. The stick is then wrapped in tissue paper and "mummified." To mummify, wrap, knot, or twist string, yarn, ribbon, etc. until it is fully covered. Use feathers, bells, beads, etc. to embellish.

3. Remind participants that the final step for this project will be to deliver their mummy to the person it is made for.

Questions for reflection or discussion

- How did it feel to make something with a specific person in mind? How did it impact the artistic choices you made?

- When you give your mummy to the recipient, will you tell them what is inside? How would you feel if they opened it to find out?

- How did it feel to make a project that was so ambiguous?

- If you were to make a series of these, how would they be similar? Different?

Meditation stones

Background

Having an object of focus can be used to aid in calming the mind in times of duress or simply as a tool to exercise the practice of mindfulness. There is a rich tradition of objects used as tools for focusing in meditation. Beginners sometimes lament the difficulty of staying focused on one thing, breath, or idea; it seems that other ideas constantly rush in, crowding our mind: "With practice, we can train the mind to stay present and focused. In yoga, we call this stage of meditation—or meditation preparation—Dhahran" (Hanoch 2016, para. 2). Experts in meditation, breath work, and mindfulness all purport that the issues of focusing and clearing the mind get easier with practice. For some people, having an object to focus on is also an approach that makes meditation more likely to be practiced.

Materials
Essentials

Stones

Materials for decorating

Scrap paper

Options and alternatives

Permanent markers

Paint pens

Acrylic paint

Collage materials and decoupage medium

Small squares of cloth

Ribbon, string, or yarn

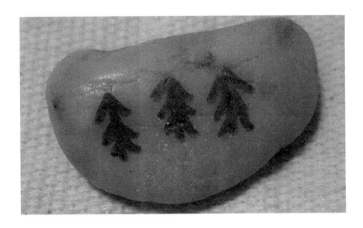

Preparation

- Procure and clean the stones you will be offering. They should be free of dirt and residue in order to offer a fresh canvas for design. The size of the stones can vary depending on participant preference and if the finished project is to be carried or placed.

- Experiment with the materials you will be offering. Stones have a variable porosity that will affect adhesion and drying time. You will be better able to guide participants based on your trials.

Process

1. Invite participants to choose the stone they would like to decorate. They may consider the size, shape, weight, or texture as they determine which stone is right for them.

2. Suggest that they spend a few minutes planning their design. Will it include a symbol of significance to them? Is there anything about the surface of the stone to work with or around? How will they make it their own? Paper and pencils for sketching are optional.

3. Using the materials provided, have participants decorate the stones. If anyone is unfamiliar with a material such as paint pens, suggest that they experiment on scrap paper first.

4. After the stone is fully dry, have participants choose a small piece of cloth to wrap their stone in. Ribbon or yarn can be used to secure the wrapping.

Questions for reflection or discussion

*   How was the experience of working on a natural surface? How did the unique traits of your stone impact your design?

*   Did you include any special symbols on your stone? Would you like to share the significance?

*   How do you plan to use your stone? If you are going to place it, where will it stay? What impact do you hope to have on the ambience of that place?

Amulet self stones

Background

Many people find comfort in carrying a small amulet in their pocket, and find that touching or rubbing it can reduce anxiety and promote relaxation. This act of touch can be soothing, increasing distress tolerance and allowing an impulse to pass or an intense emotion to dissipate. Sometimes the amulet is a stone that the person found, or a glass orb etched with an inspirational word. For this project participants make their amulet "stones" to carry.

Materials

Essentials

Oven-hardening polymer clay

Aluminum foil

Toaster or conventional oven

Options and alternatives

Salt dough or air-dry clay

Spray sealant

Preparation

- Divide the clay into portions for easy distribution.

- Precut small sheets of aluminum foil for pressing and baking the clay in.

Process

1. Explain to participants that they will be making an amulet for them to carry, a portable object of comfort. Each of their projects will be unique and should be made the size and shape that appeals to them personally.

2. Demonstrate how to begin by rolling the clay into a ball. The resulting ball should be at least as large as a marble but no larger than a ping pong ball. Depending on the materials offered, the clay might be a single color or a mix of colors, and can be mixed and marbled as desired.

3. Using the aluminum foil as a base on which the amulet will rest, participants should then gently press their thumb into the ball, flattening one side and leaving the indentation of their thumb on the other. Alternatively they can use their pointer fingers to cross in the shape of a heart.

4. Bake or allow drying as directed. Fully dried stones can then be sprayed with sealant to provide a polished look and increased durability.

Questions for reflection or discussion

- Study your own fingerprint for a few moments. What do you notice when you look at it? How does it make you feel?

- Do you have any type of talisman or charm that you carry already? When do you use it?

- Is there an activity or skill that you have been practicing that this amulet can be used in conjunction with?

Chapter 5

Books and Journals

Introduction

Book and journal projects offer a setting for a fluid back-and-forth transition between written and visual narrative. In this way they are ideal for participants who have an interest in poetry, journaling, or storytelling in addition to visual arts. Likewise, they offer the opportunity to glean insight and inspiration from overlapping therapeutic modalities.

For participants, narrative projects are a forum for recording personal stories and reflecting on them, illuminating the positives that may otherwise be overshadowed by poor self-esteem or a negative self-branding: "Counsellors and therapists engaging with narrative ideas and practices work alongside people in resisting the effects and influences of problem stories and deficit descriptions. In therapeutic conversations this involves listening and looking for clues to [knowledge] and skills that run counter to the problem-saturated story" (Narrative Therapy Centre n.d., para. 3). Participants can also use narrative projects or visual journal projects with words and art as a tool for processing difficult or traumatic content. There is some evidence that suggests that while participants may feel an immediate increase in feelings of sadness and anxiety, they may also experience an improvement in overall physical and psychological health, including a decrease in the need to seek medical care, and have a great sense of value and meaning as a result of writing (Pennebaker and Smyth 2016).

Book projects can also be used to chronicle a personal journey, lending perspective to events that unfold gradually. It is sometimes difficult to view a situation while in its midst. Journaling is a way to bear witness to incremental change: "Recording your thoughts and feelings is a testament to your life experience. We never see ourselves completely, but when we write, externalization permits you to view your thoughts and feelings. With witnessing, come new observations, reflections, and perspectives" (Reiter 2016, para. 7). The author and illustrator dictate what story gets told and how. This decision-making authority in the development of a book or journal can be exciting and empowering!

Purpose

The making of books leads to the art of writing, storytelling, creating narratives, and creative journaling. We promote the idea of journaling and storytelling with both a mix of language and visual arts, but merging creative techniques in one's book is largely a matter of personal preference. There is ample evidence to suggest that engaging in writing, telling your story, sharing an experience, or revealing traumatic memories can lead to great therapeutic benefit (Pennebaker and Smyth 2016; White and Epston 1990). In fact, it is a cornerstone of the work that so many professionals do. Book and journal projects give people the opportunity to externalize that which they carry and need to process. In many cases participants choose to engage in discussion regarding this process; however, there is benefit to be garnered from self-disclosure, even if that knowledge is not then shared. Personal insight can foster growth and healing both in the absence or presence of verbalization (Cohen and Cox 1995; Reiter 2009; White and Epston 1990).

Goals

- To provide an opportunity for participants to integrate narrative and storytelling, art, and language.

- To encourage participants to chronicle thoughts, feelings, or experience in a way that promotes self-reflection and recognition of growth over time.

- To experience journaling, writing, and/or book arts as a means of processing conscious or latent material, life experiences, and especially things that are too challenging to process verbally.

- To encourage the incorporation of text and illustration to explore identity and experience.

- To aid participants in "re-writing" their own life stories in ways that provide empowerment and encourage active participation in their own life story.

Warm-ups
Write your life story
Begin by explaining to participants that they are being given the opportunity to write and share their autobiography—their life story—but there is one essential guideline they must follow: the autobiography can only be six words long!

As an example, ask them to work together with you to create a six-word biography for a famous person. Name a celebrity or historical figure everyone in the group is familiar with, and ask them each to provide a few words that come to mind when they think of that person. For example, Cleopatra might elicit the responses: "Egyptian," "ruler," "Nile," "beauty," "history," "Rome," "loved the wrong man," or "dark horse." Use this collection to create the six-word biography, such as: "Beautiful ruler loved the wrong man."

If participants seem reluctant or intimidated by the game, spend an additional few minutes brainstorming adjectives that they might use to describe themselves or each other. Encourage reflection, self-acceptance, and humor.

Provide participants with a small piece of paper (or index card) and a writing utensil. They should spend 3–5 minutes writing their autobiographies, then invite sharing within the group (Anderson 2010). Autobiographies can be read aloud by the writer, put in a hat and read randomly by other participants, or read by the facilitator. (Choosing not to share can also be an option.)

Spend a few minutes reflecting on the activity. Ask participants: Was it fun, challenging, or frustrating? Were there any particular emotions that it brought to the forefront for you? Did you learn of anything you have in common with others in the group? Is there a way that you might incorporate this activity into today's art making?

Picture the finish line

The idea that the visualization of success can help lead to success is longstanding, and there is a growing body of science to support it:

> Brain studies now reveal that thoughts produce the same mental instructions as actions. Mental imagery impacts many cognitive processes in the brain: motor control, attention, perception, planning, and memory. So the brain is getting trained for actual performance during visualization. It's been found that mental practices can enhance motivation, increase confidence and self-efficacy, improve motor performance, prime your brain for success, and increase states of flow. (Adams 2009, para. 5)

This warm-up activity guides participants in tapping into this potential source of momentum towards achieving their personal goals.

Begin by asking participants to spend a few moments thinking of a goal they are working to reach or achieve, and explain that the visualization activity they will be doing will involve crossing the finish line to succeed in that goal.

In your own words and in a measured pace, ask participants to find a comfortable position and to close their eyes or lower their gaze, whichever they are comfortable with. Invite them to consider the goal that they are working to achieve and bring to their mind's eye the sight of a finish line where that goal has been achieved. Guide them in imagining with all of their senses: what the scene looks like, the sounds they hear, the smell in the air, the taste in their mouth, and the physical sensations they experience. Encourage them to let any doubts drift away, focusing only on success and crossing that finish line. Ask them to notice as much detail as they can, committing the scene to memory so that they can come back to that mental space again in the future, then let it slowly fade from their mind's eye. As the image dissipates, they should notice their body, their breathing, and their surroundings, opening or raising their eyes as they feel ready.

Spend a few minutes reflecting on the activity. Ask participants: Was it difficult or easy to conjure the vision initially? Were you able to remain mindful and focused throughout the visualization? If your mind strayed, how did you refocus your attention? What emotions did you experience throughout the activity? Do you think it would be useful for you to practice this same visualization again? When might you do so?

Altered books

Background

An altered book is an art piece that has been created from a single printed book, and it may include many works of art within it (Vollrath 2014). Altered books are frequently used in art therapy in part because they are fun, versatile, and lend themselves to individual personalization. They are also a popular kind of project since they lend themselves so well to the metaphors of change that we can bring to clients in therapy. Like old books, some clients feel unnecessary, useless, and disposed of. Some may feel that their story has already been written. Altered book projects lend themselves to a retelling of stories, a recycling of something that may have once held value, insight, and depth (Chilton 2007, 2013; Cobb and Negash 2010; Vollrath 2014). Altered books challenge artists to find or make a new value from something otherwise deemed worthless. This can be an ultimate challenge in therapy and life, most especially for people suffering from low self-esteem or post-traumatic stress.

Altered books can be added to over an extended period of time, making them well suited for long-term clients. They can also be short and episodic, perhaps by using children's books or pamphlets that tend to have fewer pages. Each artist gets to erase or define the rules in this project.

We think the best books for altering are hardcover books with sewn-in pages. They can be old and worn, but should maintain structural integrity, unless, of course, redefining the structural integrity is part of your artistic vision.

Some participants may be apprehensive that they are ruining a book. To the contrary, we consider this as rescuing books, saving them from disposal, and transforming them into works of art (Chilton 2007, 2013; Cobb and Negash 2010; Vollrath 2014).

CULTURAL CONSIDERATIONS: SACRED TEXTS

You may want to discourage (or eliminate from selection, if you are providing the books) the use of any books considered holy, such as the Bible or Quran. These may be triggering to different people, and some may see this as a sign of disrespect, regardless of the artist's intent. In work with an individual client, this might be less of a concern, and, in fact, clients working on some issues in therapy (e.g. religious persecution, mistrust of religious figures or texts) may find specific books to be an inspiring choice. Productive and effective group work can happen when a facilitator is mindful about the choices they make. Part of the discussion with a client or group might involve asking about what book they chose and why.

Materials
Essentials

Book for altering

Pens

Markers, pencils, drawing utensils

Glue sticks

Various materials to alter with

Options and alternatives

Magazines

Construction paper

Wrapping paper scraps

Scissors

Utility knife

Ruler

Gesso

Paint brushes

Paint

Colored tape

Decorative tape

Stamps and stamp pads

Hole and shape punches

Needle and thread or yarn

Preparation

- Procure a number of books for participants to choose from. Books should ideally be hardcover, structurally sound, and have a sewn binding (although you can create a hardcover out of cardboard or wood and attach it to a paperback with strong glue). You can identify a sewn bind by looking at the end of the book's spine—a glued binding will appear smooth, while a sewn binding will appear scalloped. The scalloped look is created by the signatures—bundles of pages folded and stitched to the spine together. You may also be able to spot the actual threads used for binding at the center of each signature within a book.

Process

1. Invite participants to choose a book. Some considerations when choosing might be the size, the way the pages feel, and the original content of the book.

2. Explain that they will need to prepare the book for altering by thinning it. This is done by removing a portion of the pages in order to make space for the elements to be added.

3. Demonstrate how pages are removed: hold the ruler close to the gutter of the page and rip or cut a few loose at a time. A small tab should remain after the page is removed. A pattern of removing three and leaving two will create ample room for altering. Remind participants to take care not to remove any images that they hope to alter.

4. While participants are thinning their book, share different techniques that can be used to alter the books. This will help you to gauge interest and customize future art-making experiences.

5. After thinning, have the participants prepare the first few pages they will be working on. This can be done by gluing

pages together in pairs with a glue stick, increasing their durability and helping to prevent materials from bleeding through on to subsequent pages. Pages can also be coated with gesso to obscure the original content and to create a blank canvas for new art.

6. Invite participants to alter their pages. We suggest that the cover be done last—a book may go through many transformations before it is finished, and cover artwork might be accidentally damaged while working on other pages.

ALTERED VARIATIONS: A FEW WAYS TO ALTER A PAGE

- Collage with words and images

- Embroider a design with a needle and floss

- Create a knock-out poem using words and phrases from the page and a bold marker to cover all the text that is not poem-worthy

- Cover with gesso then paint on a fresh canvas

- Cut out a window to show a portion of the next page

- Attach an envelope for keeping things

- Make a pop-up page

- Use decorative punches

- Sew on fabric, buttons, or other embellishments

- Cut slits and weave in paper strips

- Make a page that folds out

- Use rubber stamps

- Write a letter to yourself

- Decoupage with tissue paper

- Draw with correction fluid

- Make a design out of feathers

- Cut a page into a silhouette

- Stencil images or words

- Imbed something between two pages and then secure them closed

- Drip paint then close the page and open it again

- Doodle

Questions for reflection or discussion

- How did it feel to remove pages from the book? To draw or write in the book? Did that change at all as you prepared your book? If so, in what way?

- Did you leave any specific pages? What were you drawn to on them?

- Have you planned a specific theme for your book? If so, is there a technique or medium you feel would aid in advancing that theme?

BONUS ACTIVITY: A LETTER TO YOUR FUTURE SELF

Giving your future self the benefit of wisdom from your younger self can be a unique and special gift. The way to do this is to write (or draw, or collage!) a letter to yourself that you will only read at some predetermined time in the future. Ask a trusted friend to mail it to you, hide it at the back of your closet, or simply seal an envelope and drop it in the mail to yourself at some point a year or two or ten down the road.

Here are some ideas of what to include:

- The basics: How old you are, where you live, what you currently do regularly (school/work), etc.

- Something that you hope that you will always do

- Something that you hope you will outgrow

- Something that you aspire to become

- Advice on staying young, or advice on what to hold on to while aging

- How you hope to change the world

- Where you hope to be in the future, in five years, in ten years

- Something that is important to you now that people say you will forget or not care about in the future

- Contact information for someone you hope to stay in touch with for your whole life

- Your thoughts on a big problem (e.g. cancer, home-lessness, poverty) that hasn't been solved yet but you hope will be in the future

- Parenting tips

Accordion book personal map

Background

A map is a diagrammatic representation of an area. With personal maps, that area may be real or imaginary, literal or figurative. Some possible themes are: a plan or record of the journey to improved mental health, a map highlighting places and people of significance, or a map of your own best self, demarking positive qualities and characteristics.

Because of their size, these accordion books are suitable for easy carry in a pocket, purse, wallet, or cell phone case as an object of personal affirmation or inspiration.

Materials
Essentials

12" x 18" white construction paper (makes six pages)

or

8½" x 14" white legal-size copy paper (makes four pages)

Card stock for covers*

Magazines

Assorted collage materials including maps

Markers, pens, colored pencils

Glue sticks

Scissors

---

* Alternate material suggestions for covers: expired metro or parking cards, faux or expired credit cards, cereal box cardboard, or index cards.

Preparation

- Cut paper into strips 2" x 18" or 2" x 14" for pages, then prefold accordion style into 2 x 3 pages.

- Cut (2) 2 x 3 pieces of cardstock for covers.

- Precut images and words help to alleviate the distraction that full magazines sometimes present.

Process

1. Invite participants to first consider the theme of their map. What significant places or events do they want to include? Will they incorporate a key or ledger? If so, what types of symbols will they use?

2. Guide participants in folding pages so that they make a 2" x 3" stack, then glue on the front and back covers. Set aside to dry.

3. While the map surface is drying, participants can choose and collect the images and words they would like to use on their map. Encourage them to experiment with composition, considering what order provides the clearest directions and highlights special attractions. Remember that images can be layered and labeled.

4. Instruct participants to glue the images onto their map pages, remaining mindful of where the map folds. Images that overlap a fold a small amount are more likely to come unstuck than those that overlap completely. Remind them that they can decorate the covers too.

5. Offer markers, pens, or colored pencils to add drawings, symbols, words, or even a whole poem to their map.

6. The map should be left open to dry and gently refolded the first time after it has dried.

Questions for reflection or discussion

- Take me on a journey through your map. What sights do you want me to be sure to notice? Is there any place you hope we speed by? Why?

- Notice the scale of different features on your map. How does it impact the way the map is read?

- Does your map illustrate a specific path? Can it be traversed in different directions?

- Did you include any places to avoid? Why, or why not?

Story scrolls

Background

Hand scrolls are thought to have originated in India and were then adopted throughout Eastern Asia. They were transmitted from China to Japan in the 6th or 7th century. The art form flourished in Japan, where they depicted religious stories and folktales, recounting battles and love stories.

East Asian story scrolls are read from right to left and, similar to a book, are not designed to be viewed all at one time. They vary in size but on average are about 1 foot wide and 30 feet long. To read them, an arm's length of the scroll is rolled out at a time, allowing for the narrative to be a journey in visual space in addition to the timeline of the story (Asia Society 2018; CAEA 2018; Delbanco 2008).

Materials
Essentials

12" x 18" rice paper*	Watercolors
¼" or ½" x 12" dowels**	Brushes
Pencils	Glue stick
Ultra-fine or fine-tip permanent markers	Ribbon or string
	Ruler or straight edge

Options and alternatives

Paper	Found sticks
Paper towel tubes	

*   This project will be handled a lot, being rolled and unrolled to work and view, so a key consideration is how durable the paper will be. While rice paper is ideal, nearly any kind of paper can be substituted.

When doing so we suggest you experiment in advance, taking durability into consideration.

** You can substitute paper tubes or found sticks that are straight to use for the end spools. Just be sure to adjust your initial and final "no draw zone" to accommodate the circumference.

Preparation

- The length of the scroll will depend greatly on the length of time available and the type of story being told. Story scrolls are very well suited for multiple sessions. We suggest that scrolls be no less than 36" (two 12" x 18" sheets).

- Depending on the participants, you may choose to prepare rice paper with "no show zones" in advance. These are the spaces where the sheets will attach to the spools and each other. "No show zone" areas can be utilized by participants to obscure content they do not want to be seen or discovered. Marking these areas in advance serves to narrow the picture plane closer to dimensions participants are more accustomed to. This is helpful for participants who may find the oversized paper daunting.

- Familiarize yourself with how a story scroll is read. Unlike the texts we are accustomed to, East Asian scrolls are read from right to left. The paper begins wrapped to the left and is wound around the right spool as it is read. A length of 12"–15" remains between the spools showing the "page" or portion of the story being read.

- As the story scroll is long and expected to move as you wind the scroll around the spools, you are not going to see the entire story at once, by design. This fact lends this project well to having a discussion about not seeing the whole story at once, and having it unfold slowly over time. Factors like suspense, mystery, and anticipation come into play in this style of storytelling; these can be useful tools in learning about sequencing, cause and effect, action, consequence, responsibility, and differing character perspectives.

- The University of Chicago Center for Art of East Asia website[1] includes a number of scroll paintings that have been uploaded for public view. These can be viewed in advance or shared with participants as a visual reference (CAEA 2018).

Process

1. Introduce the project by sharing, in your own words, a little bit about East Asian story scrolls. Be sure to mention their structure and how they are read.

2. Ask participants to consider the story that they will tell on their scroll. You may have decided this in advance or allow the theme to be self-directed. A few ideas we suggest include:

   - An event from different perspectives (as an individual or a collaborative project by multiple family members).

   - An ongoing journal or the story of a single day.

   - An epic battle against an adversary that embodies personal struggle.

   - Setting a goal for the future (the last picture frame) and imagining the path to reach it.

   - Seasons of the year, with a self-portrait in each.

3. Invite participants to sketch or write out a simple plan on the copy paper. Suggest that they identify the parts of their story: setting, characters, key events, etc. If working collaboratively, ask them to identify how they will be dividing tasks, taking care that all voices in the group are heard.

---

1   https://scrolls.uchicago.edu

4. Once they are settled on a plan, provide participants with rice paper. In pencil they should faintly demark a "no show zone" of approximately 2" at both ends of the first panel. This will provide a space where the sheet will attach to the spool (right) and the following sheet (left). For all following sheets only a single "no show zone" needs to be indicated on the left. We also suggest that the orientation be marked so that unintended inversions are avoided.

5. Direct participants to sketch out their story (or portion thereof) in pencil. We suggest that light pressure be used as it is easier to alter or cover in the following steps. Once completed, offer the permanent markers for tracing.

6. Suggest participants use the bit of the "no show zone" or a separate sheet of rice paper for materials exploration before they begin tracing. They can test materials and techniques in this way any time through the process.

7. After the drawing has been inked, provide participants with watercolor paints to add color. Note that wet paper has compromised integrity. Be especially careful in handling the scroll at this point in the process. Unintended pools of water can be wicked up from the image surface by gently touching them with the corner of a paper towel.

8. After the first panel is completed, participants can attach it to the starting spool. This is done by applying glue to the "no show zone" at the right side of the image; the dowel is then rolled to the left, wrapping the paper to it like a spool. (It can be helpful to demonstrate this step.) Subsequent panels are added by gluing them atop of the existing panel's "no show zone." The scroll is completed by gluing the dowel to the last panel, rolling the paper around it to the right.

9. Finally, have participants choose a length of ribbon or string to hold their story scroll closed when it is not being read.

Questions for reflection or discussion

- Did your story change at all as you were working on it? In what ways? What do you think influenced the evolution?

- How was it to assemble your story? How does seeing the panels individually versus together alter the perspective?

- How would your story be different if read from left to right? What would you do if someone began viewing it that way? What emotions might you experience?

Simple blank books

Background

Have you ever taken note of the difference in size between construction paper and copy paper? This project takes advantage of that variation to create a super-simple book with a finished look.

Materials

Construction paper   Stapler

Copy paper   Glue stick

Scissors

Preparation

- Precut 3" x 9" strips of construction paper.

Process

1. Have participants fold five sheets of copy paper and one sheet of construction paper in half horizontally, then tuck the copy paper inside the construction paper, making sure that the open sides correspond; they should be stapled together at the folded edge. The staple should be close to the edge—be sure to catch all of the pages.

2. Next they should fold the 3" x 9" strip of a different color construction paper in half vertically, and glue over the spine edge of the book, covering the staples.

3. That's it! Participants can now use this as a sketchbook, journal, chapbook, or whatever type of book they would like it to be.

MATERIALS

We are based in the Mid-Atlantic region of the US, but our experiences and our connections crisscross the globe. From our vantage point it is pretty clear that we are far from alone in our quest to economically source supplies for artistic endeavors. Accordingly we have made sure to include resources and ideas that are not specific to any location.

It is increasingly common to find organizations and groups that collect and redistribute cheap or free art materials and resources. Sometimes you can network with other artists and teachers to find them, or consider searching the internet for keywords like recycled art, reclaimed art materials, free materials for artists/teachers, [city] recycled art, or reuse center. We have included a recommended list of these resource locations by country and state/county as Appendix 1. The ideas and recommendations in the following pages will work for you in any locale.

Chapter 6

Materials Bought, Found, Recycled, and Solicited

What to buy, when to buy

In many instances there is only a small budget for "traditional" art supplies or things generally sold in art supply stores. If this is your situation, what should you spend it on? Our recommendation is for things that stick and things that shine. These can be difficult to source as free or recycled, yet are essential tools for art making.

Adhesives are an essential component of many projects. They are, quite literally, what holds the whole thing together. Using the right adhesive for the project's materials is important. Tacky glue, glue sticks, hot glue, glue dots, spray adhesive, decoupage medium, masking tape, clear tape, packing tape—there would not be such a wide variety if they could all be used the same way. Not all adhesives are created equal. Consider the attributes of materials you are using as well as the intended life of the project, and then make the investment.

Have you ever noticed that things that shine have the seemingly magical capability of transforming something from just a pile of junk to a bona fide piece of art? Sometimes that shine or shimmer gives it the needed polish to be accepted as art. A small investment in items such as metallic paint, glitter glue, sequins, sparkly tape, shiny beads, iridescent paper, or day-glow colored markers is a cost-effective way to show your appreciation for the art clients make.

Deciding when to purchase these items can also have an impact on the cost. Many stores have annual back to school or holiday sales that offer the opportunity to stock up on materials you are sure to use. Post-holiday or off-season discounts can also be cost savers, especially for things that shine. Some stores carry art supplies just for specific holidays, and then look to purge the inventory instead of storing them. Almost all stores have a discontinued or discounted shelf in the back. And, of course, coupons, discount codes, and loyalty cards can be big savers too (online and in printed store circulars). Even if you are not a certified teacher, ask about teacher discounts. Their definition of teacher may be much broader than you expect. If you have the time, we recommend shopping around.

We do offer a word of caution: it can be easier to snatch up an excess of an item at a great price than it is to use it. Before you step up to the register, ask yourself these three questions:

- Do I have a plan for these items and in this quantity?
- Will these items spoil before that plan can happen?
- Do I have a place to keep them until then?

Another way to shop is with a friend or colleague. Partnering can increase your purchasing power, and decrease the price and your need to store excess materials.

Materials on the cheap (if not free)

Businesses go through a wealth of materials, frequently within a single material domain. They often have leftover stock or overstock, and their sales generate many waste products that they frequently dispose of or will give away. The caveat is that you have to ask. Fortunately people like to make a difference. With a phone call, an email, or a casual stop in, these types of businesses will often be happy to unload stock or scrap items onto you. Once you have made a connection, relationships with these businesses are usually easy to maintain.

MIND YOUR MANNERS!

Never underestimate the power of a thank you! While people may be more than happy to give you the excess or waste from their manufacturing, they also love to be acknowledged for doing so. Thank you notes or short anecdotes shared in person are welcome compensation and are essential to maintaining a good relationship with supply donors. A donation that is not recognized may close that door to you or others from receiving donations in the future. Good deeds are worthy of applause.

- **Wood and wood scraps:** Lumber yards or other home renovation and DIY warehouses that source wood are great places to pick up small scraps and cuttings. Lumber yards cut wood to order, and that means that whatever is left and not ordered is usually tossed away. If you need wood on a regular basis, it is to your advantage to establish a relationship with a place that throws it away. Keep in mind that wood is bulky and holding it for you means giving up space. Make it easy for them by establishing a regular pick-up time.

- **Fabric (small and large trimmings):** Fabric shops similarly sell fabric in cut-to-order amounts, which means that the pile of leftover scraps is often irregular and harder to sell. As a result, many fabric stores have a free or cheap scrap bin. You can get large swatches of fabric for just $1. If your fabric store doesn't have a bin, ask. You may be able to negotiate a lower rate or an ongoing supply. Ask them about "trim and notions" (i.e. all of the things that get attached to fabric, such as sequins, buttons, fringe, ribbon, lace, cord, zippers, bows, etc.) scraps too!

- **Tiles:** Stores that sell tiles may have miscellaneous amounts left over or open cases that have been returned, if not all of it was used on a tiling job. Ask about leftover stock, mismatched extras, or open cases sold for less than retail or given away cheap. Broken stock may be yours for the taking. Again, you just have to ask. A word of caution: broken tiles are sharp! Be sure to have a crate or heavy canvas bag for transport.

- **Paint:** The color that a paint store mixes is not always the color a customer has envisioned, and these circumstances sometimes yield returned colors sold off at cheaper prices. Additionally colors go in and out of style, which means that premixed stock may be available at a deeply discounted price. If you don't see a discount rack, ask.

- **Carpet or wallpaper:** Home improvement stores and contractor warehouses have sets of promotional materials they use to show their wares. When the new wallpaper and carpet books they use for this come from the manufacturers, old books are tossed aside. Upholstery stores have swatch books like this too. Their trash is your treasure!

- **Magazines:** Magazines are probably the easiest material to get for free. People hold on to them, with the best of intentions of making a recipe or trying that DIY project. Because of this, friends and family are usually the first place to ask. You can also ask at barber shops, doctors' offices or just about anywhere with a waiting room. You could ask your local library for their old publications too. Depending on your needs, image-heavy publications such as *National Geographic* are worth paying a few dollars for and can be found in thrift shops and at flea markets.

- **Shoeboxes:** Shoe stores always have shoeboxes; just ask.

- **Maps:** Municipalities and state or local tourist bureaus frequently provide free transit, bike path, or local attraction maps. These maps can be found in rest areas, hotel lobbies, or tourist information centers and are free for the taking. Though increasingly less frequent, car rental organizations still provide maps of their local area. Maps can be fantastic materials for using in collage, especially as people frequently feel an emotional connection to locations that define home or are marked by important events.

Look what I found! (Can you guess where?)

Good stuff can be found everywhere, not just in traditional art supply stores. Consider shopping and hunting for materials in the locations below to find unique, unconventional, and affordable art supplies. Our list includes some of the treasures we have found. Keep your eyes open when shopping. You might be surprised where you find materials that inspire your next innovative project idea!

Hardware/home improvement stores

- **Paint chips:** Paint chips are those little paper samples that show you what a paint color looks like. They are offered in paint stores or in the paint section of hardware stores, and are free for the taking. These are great for using with decorative punches or to cut up for collage projects.

- **Paint:** Usually what you will find in hardware stores is of the house paint variety, and it tends to be sold in large quantities (by the gallon, or 5-gallon container). You can sometimes buy color samples in a smaller quantity, but they do sell off stock of discontinued colors for made-to-move sale prices. Also, stores will often sell their custom-mixed but rejected colors on the cheap. Ask about sale colors or a clearance rack.

- **Keys:** Deeply symbolic, keys can be used in collages, boxes, altered books, jewelry charms, or even as chimes. Hardware stores that custom cut keys will often hold on to miscut or no longer needed keys at your request. You will almost always get more than you need, and this will almost always be one of the coolest art materials you provide.

- **Wood scraps:** Wood is a natural materials choice for sculpture or assemblage. It can also be used as a canvas for paints or decoupage.

- **Packing materials:** The materials used for packing are unique and fun to use. Bubble wrap can be used for painting textures. Packing peanuts become tacky when wet and can be used to create sculptures. The foam sheeting that is used for packing dinnerware behaves similarly to a heavy paper, but has a unique texture.

- **Rocks:** Landscaping rocks, also marketed as river rocks, are an economical canvas for talisman projects or game pieces.

- **Large fabric:** When looking to work on a large scale, canvas drop cloths, rolls of burlap, deer block fabric, or plastic barrier fences can all be cost-savvy material options. The size of the weave on each varies and can accommodate everything from banner painting to latch-hook style weaving.

Kitchen accessory/home furnishing stores

- **Plastic or metal bowl:** Bowls have the obvious use of holding and mixing materials. They can also be used as forms for papier-mâché or string bowls.

- **Blender:** A blender is an essential tool for making recycled paper pulp. This can be used for sculpture, masks, talismans, and, of course, making paper.

Grocery stores

- **Coffee or tea:** Brewed coffee or tea behaves very similarly to watercolor paints. It can also be used to stain paper to give it an aged appearance.

- **Dried ground spices:** Some spices such as turmeric can be made into a paste for painting. Other spices, such as cinnamon sticks, can be included or enclosed in artworks for the scent.

- **Whole coffee beans:** Whole coffee beans can be used in mosaics, similarly to pasta or beans. They have one significant advantage over these classics: rodents and insects find them much less desirable.

- **Foil and food wrappings:** Aluminum foil can be used for faux metal embossing, mask forms, or metallic accenting.

- **Food coloring:** Food coloring is edible and contains an intensely dense pigment. These features make it an ideal choice for food-based art or for tinting other materials such as paper pulp or slime.

Restaurant supply stores

- **Catering trays:** These can be used to distribute, sort, and collect supplies or as a tray for sand play. These also work well for building mandalas—either tracing the form or using it for a three-dimensional mandala.

- **Cocktail miniatures:** Those umbrellas, swords, and tiny forks can be used to embellish or as a body for little worry dolls. Figures and accessories can fit in well to sand tray scenes.

- **Industrial-size coffee filters:** You can use these filters to transform sorrows or fears into a tie dye—write words in a washable marker, spray with water, wad and twist, then unfold, revealing a pattern. Make them into hats or fold over a string to make a bunting flag.

Parks/playground

- **Sticks:** Generally easy to find, sticks can be used to hang chimes, build doors, transform into magic wands, or become a taking stick to designate turns. The collection of sticks can be part of the activity as well.

- **Leaves:** So many ideas!

    - Put these under paper and use pencil, crayons, or pastels to do a rubbing and make leaf prints.

    - Use with a watered-down glue solution and mold around a plastic or metal bowl (covered with saran wrap), and let dry on the bowl, to create a custom leaf bowl.

    - Use leaves as collage material on cards, envelopes, paper, or in altered books.

- **Rocks:** Paint them for use in games (e.g. hopscotch, Mancala), as a charm or amulet.

- **Flowers:** Flowers can be placed flat between paper towels in a book or under heavy books, and then used as collage material. They can also be used as embellishments in temporary works, such as leaf baskets or natural material mandalas.

Florists

- **Flowers:** Florists are often happy to find a home for stock that is past its prime or trimmed in the making of arrangements.

- **Notions:** Feathers, faux butterflies, tiny gift boxes, and all sorts of paraphernalia are used in flower arranging.

Florists are sometimes willing to give away or sell extras at a deeply discounted rate.

- **Glass stones:** Frequently coming in various colors and used in floral arrangements, these can be a vibrant addition to mosaic work. They can also usually be found in dollar stores. Be sure to price compare.

Libraries

- **Books and magazines:** Libraries are often the beneficiaries of drop-off donations that are not suitable for their collections or have books that are outdated. These may be free for the asking, or available for sale at a very reasonable price.

Party supply stores

- **Paper goods:** Paper plates, cups, and bowls are handy for all kinds of things—masks, mandalas, weaving looms, paper paddles, and, of course, materials distribution, to name just a few.

- **Table covers:** Art can get messy. Table covers are good planning.

- **Seasonal goodies:** Party supply stores survive on the sales of holiday wares, and are always getting ready for the next one. In the days following a holiday, you never know what you will find! Post-Halloween is the time for masks; post-Valentine's Day you'll find hearts galore.

- **Paper streamers:** These are handy for banners or as collage material with a unique texture.

- **Votive candles:** Candles can have deeply symbolic connotations. They can be used as an object within an artwork or as a canvas for decoupage.

Office supply stores

- **Traditional art supplies:** Office stores carry pencils, markers, crayons, tape, glue, scissors, hole punches, staplers, and many other traditional supplies. They generally have large-scale back-to-school sales that make stocking up on the basics more affordable than any other time of year.

- **Paper:** Because of the sheer quantity of paper these types of stores use, they are able to offer discounts and rebates in conjunction with manufacturers. Take advantage of their buying leverage.

- **Reinforcement labels:** These are the little donut-shaped stickers used to reinforce pages in ring binders. They can be used for reinforcing any type of paper project that is being hung up, such as streamer banners. They are also a cheap alternative to googly eyes that are not a choking hazard.

- **Manila folders:** These folders are an economical alternative to card stock. They make great book covers too.

There are a bevy of things that we use all of the time that are fantastic for making art out of. Unfortunately, most of the time these things are just thrown away. Before you contribute to landfill, ocean dumping, or even a recycle bin, take a look at the list below. The items we have listed can easily be repurposed and upcycled into art.

Holding on to items that you are accustomed to discarding can seem like accumulating excess clutter, but with a little thoughtful organization, these items take up no more space than traditional art supplies. Their versatility means that they can move fast once you have an idea for what to do with them. Their commonality makes them easy to source or share them with others in your community too.

Toilet paper and paper towel rolls:

- Kaleidoscopes
- Finger puppets
- Holiday candy tubes
- Scream box appendage

- Marionettes
- Shakers
- Superhero cuffs
- Bracelets

- Personal *piñatas*
- Painting hearts
- Castle towers
- Talking sticks

Boxes (shoeboxes, jewelry boxes, cereal boxes, shirt boxes, tissue boxes, or any other boxes):

- Dioramas
- Safe spaces
- Inside/outside projects (inside is what you keep to yourself, and outside is decorated with facets of yourself that you share with the world)
- Tissue box monsters, using the opening as a mouth

- Chip board/poster board alternative
- Box guitar
- Robots
- Maze
- Marble run
- Picture frame
- Shadow puppets
- Weaving loom

Egg cartons:

- Mancala game
- Caterpillar project
- Printing blocks or stamps
- Paint pallet
- Sorting materials such as beads or buttons
- Target for a pom-pom toss game
- Flowers with chenille stems
- Fancy glasses
- Turtle shells
- Seed planters

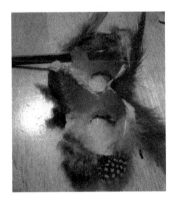

Bottle caps, juice lids, pouch food caps:

- Eyes for sculpture
- Decoration and color on junk sculptures
- Warts on the big ugly toad
- Colorful buttons on a robot or space machine
- Mosaic tiles
- Wind chimes
- Propellers
- Necklace charms
- Wheels
- Little animal bodies
- Castanets

Bottles and jars:

- Meditative glitter bottle/jar
- Layered sand art

- "Find it" jars—insert small objects or treasures into a sand or pebble media

- Mask form

- Candle holder

- Snow globe

- Bowling pin

- Wind spinner

- Rocket ship

- Vessel for a secret message

- Coin bank

- Doll body

- Yarn-wrapped vase

NETWORKING OBSTACLE: BUT I'M SHY

Problem: You're shy, you're introverted, and the idea of going into a shop where you don't know anyone and asking the manager for scraps is mortifying.

Solutions:

- Call ahead and ask on the phone, so you don't risk in person rejection if they don't have or can't give you the item you need.

- Email the business if they provide an email contact.

- Call after hours and leave a message with your contact information.

- Send a polite, typed letter to the business (and hope that they get in contact with you).

- Have your more confident friend make the call for you, and offer to share your art supply bounty.

- Don't reinvent the wheel—follow our script!

Script notes:

- Greetings! My name is [your name].

- I work for/at [school, business, organization, practice] or, I am a [insert your position].

- I am a teacher/counselor/art therapist/other who works with [people/teens/kids/seniors/veterans/ immigrants/the infirm/the community/etc.] using art as a therapeutic and educational tool.

- With a limited budget I run arts programming and am looking to procure more materials. I know that your business/organization has [insert material] and I wonder if you would be willing to give/lend/donate, etc.

- We can offer you (or your business) a note of thanks in our [exhibit program, website, group meetings, or whatever else you have access to].

THERAPEUTIC GOALS

People come to therapy to work on a large variety of things. Therapeutic goals can be as diverse and wide-ranging as people themselves. Some people know what their goals are, and some people just know that there is work to be done, even if they haven't yet identified the end goal. There are, however, some key themes that therapists do see over and over again, and some of these are things that most people grapple with at some point in their lives. In the following four chapters we discuss some of the main themes that frequently come up in therapy: safe spaces, identity exploration, trauma processing, and esteem building.

One of the things that we know to be true is that therapeutic goals can be achieved through art making. Sometimes this happens in the context of therapy or in a counselor's office, and sometimes this happens in the classroom. Still other times, this happens in a community art group, a social service setting, or a church basement. Where art happens is a lot less interesting to us than that it does happen. Research is now supporting that visual art making has beneficial psychological and physiological effects. Art making and art therapy interventions have been shown to increase self-awareness, reflection and esteem, to decrease distress, to change behavior, cognition, and patterns of thought, and to stabilize blood pressure, heart rate, and cortisol levels (Bolwerk *et al.* 2014;

Stuckey and Nobel 2010). Art therapy interventions are believed to decrease anxiety, depression, pain, and fatigue (Geue *et al.* 2010; Puetz, Morley and Herring 2013). Art therapy interventions are credited with decreasing worry, and improving communication, quality of life (Beebe, Gelfand and Bender 2010), body image and concern about future orientation (Svensk *et al.* 2009), and enhancing emotional expression (Puig *et al.* 2006). Participation in art therapy and visual art making is linked to positive personal growth, development of coping skills and increased resiliency, and the development of a new means of self-expression (Geue *et al.* 2010; Leckey 2011).

Chapter 7

Safe Spaces

Exploration of ideas pertaining to safe space is a common occurrence in therapy. People of all ages and backgrounds explore the fundamental issue of safety, both externally and internally, throughout life. Ideas pertaining to safety or a lack thereof are frequently explored in psychotherapy as well as in art (Cruz 2014; Karabanow and Naylor 2015; Tanap 2017), and may refer to a literal lack of safety, or to a metaphor for a feeling inside oneself.

Safety is a concept discussed in psychology by many prominent figures including Abraham Maslow, who included it as the second level of his infamous hierarchy of needs theory. Maslow (1943) posited that safety is so important that without first addressing an individual's safety and security needs, which may pertain to their housing, community, climate, family, or financial security, a person would be unlikely to have the emotional and psychological resources to attend to other higher order personal needs that address socialization, connectedness, intimacy, love, and self-esteem.

Safety and security are tied to an environmental dimension, and for many clients in therapy, they may have lived in or still live in unsafe circumstances. In therapy, we address issues of safety with clients who have lived through natural disasters, man-made disaster zones such as are due to war, family violence, or child abuse. Clients frequently come in bearing the fruits of intergenerational or transgenerational trauma, and thus they have a memory of or fear that one day, things will not be safe, even if they are right now. Many clients live with the absence of economic safety, which can appear as being food insecure, welfare dependent, living in poverty, and lacking basic needs such as clean running water, access to roads, work and educational opportunities.

Psychological safety is an important ingredient for a person to confidently engage in risk taking that leads to personal growth. It allows for a person to be able to show their true self, without fearing negative social or practical consequences (Winnicott 1965). Issues concerning psychological safety emerge frequently in therapy, such as with clients who are victims or witnesses to violent crime, or with clients who have a secret personal identity. Therapy frequently provides a literal safe space to explore past or current abuses, injustices, or fears of rejection of hurt. Art can also provide a space of safety for individuals to grow and to explore themselves. In fact, the main goal at the start of therapy is to create a safe space for self-expression, which helps "elicit the maximum amount of information about the client as possible so that treatment goals may be developed and pursued" (Raffaelli and Hartzell 2016, p.26). A lack of safety, real or perceived, can lead to unmanageable affect and aggression, broken attachments, alienation, extreme anxiety, insecurity, depression, uncertainty, substance abuse, and in extreme cases, even suicide (Bloom 1997, 2004a, b, 2005, 2006; Johnson 1987; Winnicott 1975).

Therapists work hard to create a safe space, sometimes using art to delineate or define that space, and frequently using art as a tool to help clients carry that defined safe space into their lives. There is some research that suggests that the implementation of art therapy in treatment can help alleviate post-traumatic stress symptoms (Chapman *et al.* 2001; Cicione, Fontaine and Williams 2002; Gantt and Tinnin 2007; Lahad *et al.* 2010; Lyshak-Stelzer *et al.* 2007; Schreier *et al.* 2005).

Establishing safety within one's own body and mind can be very difficult. This requires, in part, establishing a connection with oneself. This must allow for the ability to know one's own fears and responses, and for the development of intuition, respect for sensation, and a willingness to trust one's own wisdom (The Breathe Network n.d.). This sort of nuanced self-development can often happen through the creative process (Rappaport 1998). Art therapists and teaching artists often engage this creative process as a way of knowing the self and promoting change.

In Section 1 of this book we identified projects designed to help address many goals frequently set in therapy. Chapter 1 explored mask making, which can help a person establish the boundaries of a safe place, and distinguish what safety feels like in comparison to a lack of safety. Masks can be a physical tool allowing a person to attain safety, perhaps when wearing a mask (which can be representative of another identity), or perhaps when removing the mask to reveal the true self: "Clients may use...masks to speak for them; they may hide behind them in order to feel safer when sharing" (Buchalter 2009, p.125). A person might find greater safety behind the mask where the true self is concealed. What matters is not where an individual finds safety, but that the mask can become a tool for exploring the phenomenon of seeking and possibly finding or establishing safety.

In Chapter 3 of this book we explored the use of boxes in therapy, which can provide a figurative or literal safe space. Boxes can be explored in the realms of reality or fantasy, and are containers by design; things can be enclosed within or kept out. Box projects are commonly used in art education and art therapy realms, and provide easy metaphors to the self by considering the box from the inside and the outside, the functions of opening and closing, as well as factors such as sturdiness, accessibility, containment, and visibility. Some projects that use boxes include the making of dioramas, safe houses (Leasure 2017; Rappaport 1998), memory boxes, Pandora's box or a box of secrets, time capsules, or representations of the self and one's values, aspects, or traits (Klammer n.d.; Makin 2000).

Chapter 8

Identity Exploration

Knowing oneself, understanding personal traits, and having an appreciation of the enduring characteristics that make up one's personality can help individuals to feel secure in life. Exploring one's identity can be an important component for clients in therapy at any age, and especially in the wake of growth or changes that have transpired in life. Identity exploration can involve many facets of knowing the self, including likes and dislikes, preferences and tendencies, connections to or relationships with others, goals, dreams, and life plans.

People who know themselves and feel a connection to and respect for who they are seem to have an easier time navigating the ups and downs of life. There is a large part of life that is defined by identity exploration: we call this adolescence. There is some research that suggests that this process now continues well into early adulthood. Identity exploration can emerge as a goal at any point in life and is frequently needed after an individual sustains a major life change. People have a need to reaffirm or reestablish "who am I now?"

Many art therapists, counselors, art educators, and other helping professionals assist in facilitating clients' journeys of better knowing and owning themselves. There is no one right way to do this. Guest (2017) has designed a workbook with creative activity sheets that can be used as visual art or writing prompts, and that are intended to help people explore their own identity and better know themselves. She puts forth various activities to help an individual address their family history, prominent developmental influences, sexuality and gender, values, emotional wellbeing, problems, decision-making ability, future, emotions, and inner experiences (Guest 2017).

Identity development and exploration is important at all stages of life. Kramer (1971) wrote about art as a tool for identity development and understanding in children. She posited, "art is a means of supporting the ego, fostering the development of a sense of identity, and promoting maturation in general" (1971, p.xiii). Erikson (1980) wrote about the crisis of identity and the resulting role confusion that is inherent in adolescence, in part based on the extreme mental, physical, and social changes that typify that life stage. Piaget (1951) noted that cognitive development around adolescence is marked by brain development and moral changes that tend to have people questioning what they believe, as a facet of who they are. These types of normative developmental shifts can necessitate revisiting of one's own identity at multiple points in life.

Identity exploration, or knowing oneself, is often written about in therapeutic literature as self-awareness. Coholic (2010) writes about the development of self-awareness in youth through art making. She uses activities such as feelings collage and inventory, feelings bracelets, stream of consciousness writing, journals, mantras, and tree drawings to bring a greater sense of awareness to identity and identity development. These activities aim to increase the self-esteem of children and adolescents (Coholic 2010). Buchalter (2011) writes about the use of art therapy techniques with older adults who are working on increasing self-awareness, knowing that people change throughout life as they grow and shift into new identities. These activities frame aging as a time for personal growth and restoration, and remind users that any stage of life can be right for personal investigation and self-study.

Some media and art directives lend themselves to exploration of identity, such as the creation of masks and dolls

(Feen-Calligan, McIntyre and Sands-Goldstein 2009), the use of collage (Malone and Rosal 1993), or personal symbols such as a coat of arms or flags (Buchalter 2009). Some activities, like journal writing or response drawing, lend themself to introspection and personal exploration (Makin 2000). Art and writing directives that address components of ourselves—such as what we like to do, important moments in our lives, a favorite place, season, or activity—help us to explore and ultimately better know ourselves.

In this book, Chapter 1 explored mask making, which can help a person investigate their own identity, and how that compares to desired or respected identities. Stepping into a mask and subsequently a character allows for exploring the identity one has, as well as the identity one wants, or aspects of identity that they might seek to incorporate into their own. It is sometimes through knowing other people that we can better know ourselves.

In the world of fine art, mask making has a role in facilitating identity exploration (Knight 2016; Schwartz n.d.; Zwicky 2010). In the world of art therapy, we see identity as a dual process, consisting of the aspects of self that we promote, put forth, and share with others, and also the identity we internalize and keep hidden. The dual-sided surfaces of masks are sometimes used to give form to those two facets (Brumleve n.d.; Corrington 2012; Kaimal 2017), which may be drastically different, as is the case sometimes, or may have great similarity. Either way, processing the appearance of the mask and the meaning behind it can be an eye-opening exercise.

Kaimal (2017) discusses a research study that examined and analyzed masks made in art therapy by active duty service men and women. The researchers found that the masks suggested "visual representations of the self related to individual personhood, relationships, community and society" (Walker et al. 2017). Imagery referenced traumatic experiences, relationships, loss, and resiliency. This study has highlighted the experiences of service members, but it has also shown some of the possibilities for exploring the self over time and under various circumstances through mask art (Walker et al. 2017).

Chapter 9

Trauma Processing

Therapy can be a natural and useful place for addressing trauma symptoms and history and processing that trauma. In many cases, clients are processing their trauma long before they realize that is what they are doing, or that it might even be a goal. We consider trauma processing to be long-term work, with long-range goals. This is due in part to the sustained presence of traumatic memories and symptoms, even if the trauma itself was a single incident.

Processing of past traumatic experiences, sustained life events, or memories associated with trauma has many layers. Individuals may benefit from identifying trauma experiences, memories, or causes, and sometimes from naming these issues. Some clients need not name traumatic memories or causes, but just giving form, voice, art, or shape to them is significant. Expressing trauma through art can be immensely healing—sometimes immediately, and sometimes with delayed gratification. Clients frequently feel unburdened when the trauma that they have been carrying is externalized through art; through this acknowledgement, it may no longer be necessary to carry it as they have before (Johnson 1987).

It is important to state, though, that processing a trauma is not always a goal for clients, and may, in fact, be contraindicated (Kraybill 2018). For a select group of clients, bringing out their trauma experiences may do more harm than good, which is why it is important to work with a trained mental health professional. There are many things you should consider before engaging in trauma processing or encouraging a person to process their trauma experiences; one factor to consider is if this is in your scope of professional skills, identity, experience, and role. It would likely be considered ethically irresponsible to dive into an excavation of trauma symptoms and experiences in a first therapeutic session, for example. That same client might be ready and able to tackle that tough material after first establishing a trusting relationship and safety within therapy. When processing trauma, establishing a sense of stability and safety is a primary concern. A secondary concern is to make sure that symptoms are properly managed, and that coping skills have been established and implemented.

Part of achieving safety is to establish a trusted rapport before exploration of trauma in therapy. We sometimes believe that simply telling a trauma story is all that is needed to bring relief. Indeed, in some instances this may be true. But telling a trauma story can also be re-traumatizing (Kraybill 2018); that is, telling a trauma story may incite the very feelings and symptoms that perpetuate a person's traumatic response. As traumatic memories are not always stored in a linear, logical, organized, cognitive pattern, it can be difficult to explore and relieve symptoms of trauma through an organized narration (Johnson 1987). Stories of trauma often come out in associative ways that put weighty thoughts and feelings before chronology in narration.

Trauma experiences and memory are stored in the body. These "disruptive consequences play out in sensory networks, the nervous system and the vagus nerve that connect many parts of the body including the brain and the gut" (Kraybill 2018). Treating trauma is complex and means involving all of the body systems, which can happen through creative practice. Survivors of trauma frequently need to first address their heightened state of alert, which helps fortify them against further trauma, but also may block paths to processing the trauma and healing hurt (Hargrave-Nykaza 1994; Johnson 1987). Ochberg (1991) writes about the importance of post-traumatic therapy, and the importance of this in helping clients to show fewer post-trauma symptoms, develop a sense of control in their life, and shift their status from victim to survivor. He discusses four categories of work done in therapy with victimized clients who display post-traumatic symptoms; they include therapy, enhancing social support and integration, education, which may pertain to legal, biological or psychological aspects of their trauma, and holistic health issues, which could include physical activity, sleep, nutrition, spirituality, creativity, or humor (Ochberg 1991).

Jones (2018) says that social services interventions will not help unless trauma is confronted, which can mean confronting traumatic events, memories, post-trauma symptoms, and the after-effects that make it hard for people to hold on to jobs, relationships and homes: "[Trauma] sabotages early successes" (Jones 2018, para. 4).

Clients who have experienced adverse circumstances likely seen as traumatic frequently have intrusive imagery in the form of memories, flashbacks, dreams, or nightmares. This is commonly seen with individuals who have sustained child sexual abuse or other sexual abuse trauma such as forced prostitution or trafficking. Intrusive imagery can sometimes be the trigger for affect-related symptoms or disorders, and harnessing control over that imagery can feel impossible. One treatment approach varied art materials and tasks as a means of engaging with past trauma (Peacock 1991). Alternating "fluid expression with controlled problem solving tasks" (Peacock 1991, p.104) seemed to suggest positive changes.

Eventual processing of trauma means starting with establishing a real and perceived sense of safety, and identifying resources, tools, and coping strategies. Art can help in this process. For some people, art can provide a sort of road map for navigating memories, symptoms, or a traumatic response (Yates and Pawley 1987). In addition to using art to process real trauma, it can be used to identify and create tools (Hargrave-Nykaza 1994). Art projects that can help to identify resources and tools for coping include journals (Luckett 2011), diaries, letter writing, altered books, scream boxes, self-care vessels, resource jars, puzzles, and meditation tools such as glitter bottles (Klammer n.d.).

Chapter 10

Esteem Building

Esteem building in therapy has many components that include knowing self, respecting self, valuing self, and liking self. The frequency with which this goal is set in therapy does not make it any easier to achieve within an individual client. This goal requires that we ask difficult questions, such as, what makes people feel good about themselves? And what causes people to not value themselves? It could be argued that it takes a long time to learn to love yourself, and this statement sometimes feels more true in the face of trauma. Frequently, individuals are working to overcome issues of shame, guilt, and regret, in order to then like themselves. But people are resilient, and they can, in fact, learn to like themselves. This is worth it, too, as sustained self-esteem helps to bolster resiliency and can lessen instances of depression and suicide.

In art therapy, one way that we develop and increase esteem is through the establishment of an artist identity. The act of creation typically results in a certain degree of pride, something we see naturally exhibited in healthy children who love to proclaim, "I made this!" We see it less in adolescents and adults who don't want to brag or show off, or may even view creative efforts as ordinary or not special. Creative pursuits need not be unique to be celebrated. Each person's attempts at creativity can be celebrated. Clients in art therapy frequently take pride in creation, skill development, gained mastery, and even risk taking. Trying something new requires one to take a risk. Construction, collaboration, and expression all require the willingness to try, and this can be the start of identifying change in identity and action for a person.

A natural remedy for confronting low self-esteem is addressing areas where a person feels some degree of weakness. This is frequently in the area of art. Art therapists frequently hear common refrains such as, "I'm not an artist," "I don't know how to draw," and "I can only draw a stick figure." When I hear such excuses, explanations, and defenses I am reminded of how uncomfortable people feel when flexing new muscles and forging into uncharted territories. For most of us, as soon as we try something new, such as making art, the inner critic is right there, witnessing our attempts with disdain. Your inner critic, also known as the voice in your head, your self-saboteur, or your inner demon, is fantastic at justifying why you suck and should not even be trying that potentially amazing new thing that you're trying: "Part of getting past the demons to the creativity and the making of stuff is accepting that the demons exist and learning to cope with them" (Werker 2014, introduction). Getting past the demons is part of the work of the art therapist or facilitator, and it is part of the work of increasing self-esteem by trying new things and taking calculated risks. Nothing builds an artist identity like making art—good art, bad art, complicated art, simple art, misunderstood art, thought-provoking art, or any art at all.

Two of the most common and popular techniques for addressing self-esteem, as well as other issues in therapy, are cognitive behavioral therapy (CBT) and dialectical behavioral therapy (DBT). Both of these approaches deal with the intersection of emotions, thoughts, and behaviors, and it is not uncommon to see CBT or DBT merged with art therapy. Behaving as an artist, or making art, can sometimes help us think and feel like a creator, a creative person, and one who can problem-solve and make change as needed. Aaron Beck initiated CBT in the 1960s, and believed that clients could exert greater control over their anxiety with increased self-awareness and thought control. This approach attempts to slow down and understand the thought process so as to initiate change. Clients learn that their thoughts affect their feelings and vice versa, both affect behaviors. There is an emphasis on transforming thought patterns towards positivity, and by reducing stress and anxiety, also increase self-esteem. As clients are encouraged to take control of their own thoughts, art can be a useful outcome in exploring thoughts, feelings, and behaviors, both real and ideal. Marsha Linehan created DBT in the 1970s as a way of helping facilitate a future orientation in clients. Clients' experience is validated as they define where they are in the present and where they would like to be, as well as a path to get there. Together the therapist and client identify dreams and goals that become a road map for the therapy, and give the client a specific idea of what they are working towards. A major part of DBT is helping clients to understand and be able to hold two, possibly-conflicting realities simultaneously, and to force less stressful dichotomous thought and choices. Effort is given to considering outcomes and consequences. DBT includes development of mindfulness skills, interpersonal effectiveness skills, emotion regulation skills, and distress tolerance skills. Self-soothing is an important and cultivated skill set in DBT too; our ability to calm ourselves directly affects our esteem (Buchalter 2015).

We see useful links between CBT and DBT as therapeutic techniques and the art of making masks, flags, boxes, charms, and books (Pifalo 2007). These complex approaches to healing are intended to problem-solve very real personal issues that center around self-talk and about how we deal with ourselves. In that way, they lend themselves to art making. Understanding our inner dialogue and the way we bolster or sabotage ourselves can be a key piece in working towards a more authentic self and satisfying life. These approaches identify a problem or phenomenon, and through the examination of feelings and thoughts that are associated, try to find ways of alleviating the problem. It is frequently through art work that clients can really see a problem and identify what is not working for them, or what parts of a situation need fixing.

In art therapy, a number of techniques are commonly used in assisting a client's investigation of self, development of self-respect, and ultimately in the building of their esteem (Buchalter 2015). Some approaches include using one's name or initials as a primary canvas and building art on these identity markers (Buchalter 2009). Other techniques involve creating personal advertisements, brochures, a billboard, or other products typically linked to sales and marketing (Buchalter 2009; Swank 2008); the idea is that you can't "sell" something without understanding and knowing the value of it. Another common idea is to create one's self as a superhero or another fantasy version of oneself (Buchalter 2009; Rubin 2008). This sort of intensely capable alter ego is a means of helping a person identify the things they would like to pursue, if they felt able and obstacles were removed.

Another means of helping people identify how they feel about themselves, or how their real and desired self-esteem do not equate, is through inside/outside projects (Buchalter 2009), which can be easily and successfully accomplished using a mask or a box. I have frequently encouraged clients to explore themselves by creating a self-box, and they discover and apply their own metaphor of inside and outside. Noting that there might be part of the box (or mask) that is unseen to the naked eye, without manipulating or moving things around, is an exciting discovery. Boxes and masks lend themselves well to exploring both the parts of ourselves that are exposed and the parts that we keep hidden, and this mirrors closely how many people feel, at least in some part of their life.

The creative process in itself can be fuel for self-esteem, as it reminds the self that "I can." Being a creator, a maker, an inventor of something that wasn't before, can be an empowering reality. Making art means establishing and executing ideas. It often means problem-solving, and decision-making, and moving past emotional obstacles. Buchalter (2009, p.152) writes that, "Individuals gain greater control and self-esteem as they learn how to problem-solve and accept creative challenges."

Appendix 1

Where to get materials

As artists, educators, art therapists, parents, and community members, sometimes we find a cache of unusual material and work to make the best use of it. Sometimes these are things that we are gifted. Sometimes we find them, and still other times we seek them out. Sometimes inspiration for a project or art idea is born out of the material itself (socks naturally make great puppets). And sometimes we have a project burning in us and we contort a material to fit the need (this was the case with masks made from gallon milk cartons).

Creative reuse centers are places that amass and distribute things discarded by the community and intended for creative use. Sometimes they are open to the public; others cater only to schools, non-profits, artists, or another category of registered users. They frequently accept discarded materials from various industries including manufacturing, technology, fashion, and theater. Some creative reuse centers offer actual art supplies, while others offer building or home repair supplies, bit parts, or just miscellaneous stuff.

Below are places that lend themselves well to finding unusual and unique materials, sometimes in great quantities, and often at great discounts. In some cases there are limitations to who can access these resources (you must have non-profit status in New York City to register to shop at Materials for the Arts, for example), but we think they are worth knowing about all the same. Hopefully there is a shopping venue on this list that you can visit and access, and if not, use this as inspiration to search for like venues in your neighborhood or town. This is not an exhaustive list, which is why we've included a few blank pages at the end for you to write in your own additions.

Happy material hunting!

Australia
Marrickville, New South Wales

Reverse Garbage, Experts in reuse: 8/142 Addison Road, Marrickville, NSW 2204

Tel: + 61 2 9569 3132
Email: info@reversegarbage.org.au
http://reversegarbage.org.au or www.facebook.com/RevGarb

Melbourne, Victoria

Resource Rescue Inc., Eco-friendly craft supplies: 1/42 Burgess Road, Bayswater North, VIC 3153

Tel: + 61 3 9761 5545
Email: sonia@discountcraftsupplies.com.au
https://discountcraftsupplies.com.au or www.facebook.com/resource rescuecraftsupplies

West Perth, Western Australia

REmida, Reuse community: Creative Reuse Centre, 1 Prospect Place, West Perth, WA 6003

Tel: + 61 8 9227 5576
Email: admin@remidawa.com
www.remidawa.com

Austria
Linz, Upper Austria

REmida Linz: Sperberweg 4, 4030 Linz, Austria

Tel: +43 650 466 22 00
Email: mail@reggiobildung.at
www.reggiobildung.at

Canada
Vancouver, British Columbia

Urban Source, Alternative art materials: 3126 Main Street, Vancouver, BC
V5T 3G7

Tel: +1 604 875 1611
Email: usource@shaw.ca
www.urbansource.bc.ca

Burlington, Ontario

Art Hive at Open Doors: 662 Guelph Line, Burlington, ON L7R 3M8

Tel: + 1 905 634 1809
www.stchristophersburlington.com/opendoors.html or https://arthives.
org/arthives/art-hive-open-doors

Montreal, Québec

ArtPatro: 7355 Christophe-Colomb Avenue, Montreal, QC H2R 2S5

Tel: +1 514 273 8535
Email: culturel@patroleprevost.qc.ca
http://patroleprevost.qc.ca

Concordia University, Engineering and Visual Arts Integrated Complex:
1515 Sainte-Catherine St West, Montreal, QC, H3G 2W1

Tel: + 1 514 848 2424
http://arthives.org [Includes an option to search for Art Hives in other
areas]

Le Milieu: 1251 rue Robin, Montreal, QC H2L 1W8

Tel: +1 438 932 1251
Email: info@lemilieu.ca
www.lemilieu.ca or www.facebook.com/cooplemilieu

Native Immigrant Art Hive: 5442 Cote Saint Luc (Corner of Earnscliffe),
Montreal, QC H3X 2C5

Tel: +1 514 299 4645
http://arthives.org/arthives/native-immigrant-art-hive

Wynyard, Saskatchewan

The Art Nest: Wynyard's Open Art Studio, 325 Bosworth Street, Wynyard,
SK S0A 4T0

Email Dana Stefanson: d.stefanson@outlook.ca
http://arthives.org/arthives/art-nest-wynyards-open-art-studio

Germany
Berlin

Kunst-Stoffe: Berliner Str. 17, 13189

    Tel: +49 303 408 9840

    Email: info@kunst-stoffe-berlin.de

    www.kunst-stoffe-berlin.de

Hamburg

ReMida: Am Born 19, 22765

    Tel: +49 176 510 45 798

    Email: remida@gmx.net

    www.remida.de

Italy
Torino

ReMida – Turin: Centro Remida via Tollegno 83

    Tel: +39 11 443 2001 2004

    Email: iter@comune.torino.it

    www.comune.torino.it/iter

New Zealand
Wanaka

Wanaka Wastebusters: 189 Ballantyne Road, Wanaka 9382

    Tel: +64 3 443 8606

    Email: admin@wastebusters.co.nz

    www.wastebusters.co.nz

United Kingdom: England
Bristol

Children's Scrapstore and Artrageous: Scrapstore House, 21 Sevier Street, St Werburghs, Bristol BS2 9LB

    Tel: +44 117 908 5644

    www.childrensscrapstore.co.uk or www.facebook.com/ childrensscrapstore

High Wycombe, Buckinghamshire

Wycombe Resource Zone, Community organization in High Wycombe: Unit 9, Lincoln Road, Lincoln Business Centre, Cressex Industrial Estate, High Wycombe HP12 3RD

Tel: +44 149 452 8804

Email: wrz@wycombe.gov.uk

www.facebook.com/Wycombe-Resource-Zone-408078432621397

Pool, Cornwall

Pool ScrapStore, Cornwall College (Unit 18b), Trevenson Road, Pool TR15 3RD

Tel: +44 172 682 1161

www.cornwallscrapstore.co.uk

St Austell, Cornwall

St Austell ScrapStore: Goonmarris, St Austell, PL26 7QX

Tel: +44 172 682 1161

Email: garyscrapstore@aol.com

www.cornwallscrapstore.co.uk

Exeter, Devon

Exeter Scrapstore: Belmont Park, Gordon Road, Exeter EX1 2DH

Tel: + 44 139 266 1769

Collections and Warehouse email: peter@exeterscrapstore.co.uk

Creative Workshops and Admin email: kat@exeterscrapstore.co.uk

General email: info@exeterscrapstore.co.uk

www.exeterscrapstore.co.uk

Holsworthy, Devon

Holsworthy Family Workshop and Resource Centre (HFWRC): Ground Floor, Manor Offices, Holsworthy, Devon EX22 6DJ

Tel: + 44 140 925 4272

Email: holsworthyfamilyworkshop@googlemail.com

www.hfwrc.com/index.htm

Poole, Dorset

Dorset Scrapstore: The Factory, 14 Alder Hills, Poole, Dorset BH12 4AS

Tel: +44 756 557 7094

Email: enquiries@dorsetscrapstore.org.uk

http://dorsetscrapstore.org.uk or www.facebook.com/DorsetScrapstore

London

Squirrels Community Scrap Scheme: The Old Allotment Hut, 131 Boscombe Road, Worcester Park KT4 8PJ

Tel: +44 748 492 3769

www.squirrelscommunityscrapscheme.btck.co.uk

Middlesbrough, North Yorkshire

Percy Middlesbrough Scrapstore, creative reuse center: C2 Commerce Way, Off Skippers Lane, Middlesbrough TS6 6UR

Tel: +44 164 245 6905 or +44 796 369 2424

Email: info@percymiddlesbrough.co.uk

www.percymiddlesbrough.co.uk or www.facebook.com/percymiddlesbrough

Weston-super-Mare, Somerset

Children's Scrapstore, Weston-super-Mare Satellite Store: The Motex Centre, Winterstoke Rd, Weston-super-Mare BS23 3YW

Tel: +44 193 441 6286

www.childrensscrapstore.co.uk

Brownhills, Staffordshire

Saxon Hill Craft Barn: Unit 7, Pool Road, Brownhills WS8 7NL

Tel: +44 154 337 1200

http://saxonhillcraftbarn.co.uk

Benton, Tyne and Wear

House of Objects: Rising Sun Countryside Centre, Whitley Road, Benton, Newcastle Upon Tyne NE12 9SS

Tel: +44 191 266 2269

http://houseofobjects.org

Farsley, West Yorkshire

Scrap Creative Reuse Arts Project Ltd, Creative reuse, play and learning: The Spinning Mill, Sunny Bank Mills, Paradise Street/Charles Street, Off Farsley Town Street, Farsley LS28 5UJ

Tel: +44 113 345 2627
Email: scrapenquiries@gmail.com
www.scrapstuff.co.uk

Swindon, Wiltshire

Swindon Children's Scrapstore and Resource Centre: The Scrapstore, Unit 7, Bramble Close, Elgin Industrial Estate, Swindon SN2 8DW

Tel: +44 179 351 3982
Email: swss@scrapstore.co.uk
www.scrapstore.co.uk

United Kingdom: Northern Ireland
Belfast, County Antrim

Play Resource: North City Business Centre, 2 Duncairn Gardens, Belfast BT15 2GG

Tel: +44 289 035 7540
Email: admin@playresource.org
http://playresource.org

United Kingdom: Scotland
Crieff, Perth and Kinross

Remake Scotland: Unit 2, Crieff Visitor Centre, Muthill Road, Crieff PH7 4HQ

Tel: +44 176 465 5733 or +44 750 557 6361
Email: info@remakescotland.co.uk
www.remakescotland.co.uk

United Kingdom: Wales

Re-Create: Ely Bridge Industrial Estate, Wroughton Place, Cardiff CF5 4AB

Tel: +44 29 2057 8100
www.re-create.co.uk/contact-us.html

United States
Mobile, Alabama

Gulf Regional Early Childhood Services, Inc.: 3100 Cottage Hill Road, Bldg 4 Suite 400, Mobile, AL 36606

Tel: 251 473 1060
Email: info@grecs.org
www.grecs.org/the-resource-place

Tempe, Arizona

Treasures 4 Teachers: 3025 South 48th Street, Suite 101, Tempe, AZ 85282

Tel: 480 751 1122
www.treasures4teachers.org

Fresno, California

T4T @ 2BCF: 2720 North Grove Industrial Drive #101, Fresno, CA 93727

http://twobitcircus.org/our-programs/upcycled-materials

Gardena, California

Two Bit Circus Foundation (formerly Trash for Teaching, Inc.): 12815 S. Western Avenue, Gardena, CA 90249

Tel: 310 527 7080
Email: info@twobitcircus.org
http://twobitcircus.org or http://twobitcircus.org/our-programs/steam-labs

Long Beach, California

The Long Beach Depot for Creative ReUse: 320 Elm Ave, Long Beach, CA 90802

Tel: 562 437 9999
Email: info@thelongbeachdepot.org
http://thelongbeachdepot.org

Los Angeles, California

reDiscover Center: 12958 W. Washington Blvd, Los Angeles, CA 90066

Tel: 310 393 3636
http://rediscovercenter.org

LACoMax, Materials exchange program
https://ladpw.org/epd/lacomax/default.aspx

Oakland, California

East Bay Depot for Creative Reuse: 4695 Telegraph Avenue, Oakland, CA 94609

Tel: 510 547 6470
http://creativereuse.org

Sacramento, California

ReCreate: 8417 Washington Boulevard #135, Roseville, CA 95678

Tel: 916 749 3717
www.recreate.org

San Diego, California

Art Hive at TAY: 1050 North Broadway, Building C, 92026 Escondido, CA

Tel: Candice Redden at 760 271 3147
Email Candice Redden: credden@ymca.org
https://arthives.org/arthives/art-hive-tay

San Francisco, California

SCRAP, A source for the resourceful: 801 Toland Street, San Francisco, CA 94124

Tel: 415 647 1746
Email: scrap@scrap-sf.org
www.scrap-sf.org

FabMo, Inc., Fabric and more: 970 Terra Bella Avenue, Suite 8, Mountain View, CA 94043

www.fabmo.org/fabmo/Home.html

Santa Barbara, California

Art From Scrap, Creative reuse store: 302 East Cota Street, Santa Barbara, CA 93101

Tel: 805 884 0459 Ext. 11
https://reusesb.com or https://exploreecology.org

Boulder, Colorado

ArtParts, Creative reuse center: 2870 Bluff Street, Boulder, CO 80301

Tel: 720 379 5328
www.artpartsboulder.org

Boulder Art Therapy Collective: 1400 Lee Hill Drive, #7, Boulder, CO 80304

Tel: 303 593 0277
Email: info@boulderarttherapycollective.com
www.boulderarttherapycollective.com or https://arthives.org/arthives/boulder-art-therapy-collective

Denver, Colorado

Violet Hive Art, Therapy and healing: 4956 East Colfax Avenue, Denver, CO 80220

http://violethiveart.org

New Haven, Connecticut

EcoWorks, Inc.: 262 State Street, New Haven, CT 06510

Tel: 203 498 0710
https://ecoworksct.org

Melbourne Beach, Florida

Reusable Resources Association, A nonprofit that supports the development of reusable resource centers for educators, artists, and the greater community: PO Box 511001, Melbourne Beach, FL 32951

Tel: 321 984 1018
www.reuseresources.org

Orlando, Florida

A Gift for Teaching: 6501 Magic Way, Bldg 400C, Orlando FL 32809

Tel: 407 318 3123
Email: freestore@agiftforteaching.org
www.agiftforteaching.org

Tallahassee, Florida

The Sharing Tree: 2415 North Monroe Street, Suite 1190, Tallahassee, FL 32308

Tel: 850 264 4035
Email: recycle4art@yahoo.com
http://thesharingtreefl.org

Atlanta, Georgia

WonderRoot Creative Reuse: 982 Memorial Drive SE Atlanta, GA 30316

Tel: 404 254 5955
Email: info@wonderroot.org
https://wrcratl.wordpress.com or www.wonderroot.org/public-programs/creative-reuse or https://squareup.com/store/wonderroot

Garden City, Idaho

The Reuse Market (Co-located with North End Organic Nursery and J. Michaels Florist): 3777 West Chinden Boulevard, Garden City, ID 83714

www.reusemarket.org

Champaign, Illinois

The Idea Store: 28 East Springfield Avenue, 2nd Floor, Champaign, IL 61820

Tel: 217 352 7878
http://the-idea-store.org

Welton, Iowa

Make it Yours Upcycle Center: 411 Main Street, Welton, IA 52774

Tel: 563 659 1534
www.makeityoursupcyclecenter.org

New Orleans, Louisiana

The Green Project, Creative recycling and reuse center: 2831 Marais Street, New Orleans, LA 70117

Tel: 504 945 0240
https://thegreenproject.org or http://thegreenproject.typepad.com/thegreenproject/recycle_for_the_arts

Farmington, Maine

Everyone's Resource Depot, At the University of Maine at Farmington Campus, Room 009 of the Education Center on campus, at the corner of Lincoln and High Streets

Tel: 207 778 7150

www2.umf.maine.edu/resourcedepot

Portland, Maine

Ruth's Reusable Resources: 39 Blueberry Road, Portland, ME 04102

Tel: 207 699 5565

www.ruths.org

Rockland, Maine

Midcoast Art Hive: 385 Main Street, #9, Rockland, ME 04841

Email: midcoastarthive@gmail.com

www.artloftrockland.org

Baltimore, Maryland

Reuse Development Organization, Inc. (ReDO): c/o The Loading Dock, 2 North Kresson Street, Baltimore, MD 21224

Tel: 410 558 3625 Ext. 15

Email: redo@loadingdock.org

http://loadingdock.org/redo

Boston, Maryland

Pop-Up Recycle Shop: Boston Children's Museum, 308 Congress Street, Boston, MA 02210

Tel: 617 426 6500

www.bostonchildrensmuseum.org/calendar/pop-recycle-shop

Ann Arbor, Michigan

SCRAP Box: 581 State Circle, Ann Arbor, MI 48108

Tel: 739 994 0012

https://scrapbox.org

Detroit, Michigan

Arts & Scraps: 16135 Harper, Detroit, MI 48224

Tel: 313 640 4411

www.artsandscraps.org

Grand Rapids, Michigan

Learning from Scratch: 1454 28th Street (inside the CompRenew Store), Grand Rapids, MI 49508

Tel: 616 901 7486

http://learningfromscratch.org

Wisemaker Creative Reuse Store and Studio, Reclaimed art and craft supplies and drop-off site for unwanted, usable art and craft supplies: @ The Geek Group, 902 Leonard St NW, Grand Rapids, MI

Tel: 616 466 4335

Email: kelly@thegeekgroup.org

St Paul, Minnesota

ArtScraps Reuse Store: 1459 St Clair Avenue, St Paul, MN 55105

Tel: 651 698 2787

www.artstart.org/artscraps-reuse-store

St Louis, Missouri

St Louis Teachers' Recycle Center, Inc.: South County Resource Center, STL Venture Works, 315 Lemay Ferry Road – Suite 138, St Louis, MO 63125

Tel: 636 288 4985

http://sltrc.com

Chesterfield, Missouri

Chesterfield Resource Center: Chesterfield Mall, 291 Chesterfield Mall, Ste 108, Chesterfield, MO 63017

Tel: 636 227 7095

http://sltrc.com

Albuquerque, New Mexico

OFFCenter Community Arts Project: 808 Park Avenue, SW Albuquerque, NM 87102

Tel: 505 247 1172

Email: studio808@qwestoffice.net

http://offcenterarts.org

Ithaca, New York

Ithaca ReUse Center: 214 Elmira Road, Ithaca, NY 14850

Tel: 607 257 9699

https://ithacareuse.org

New Paltz, New York

New Paltz Reuse and Recycling Center: 3 Clearwater Road, New Paltz, NY 12561

Tel: 845 255 8456

Email: recycling@townofnewpaltz.org

www.newpaltzreuse.org

Landfill & Recycling Center: 99 Clearwater Rd, New Paltz, NY 12561

Tel: 845 255 8456

New York

Materials for the Arts (MFTA): 33-00 Northern Boulevard, 3rd Floor, Long Island City, NY 11101

www.mfta.org or www.materialsforthearts.org or www.nyc.gov/html/dcla/mfta/html/home/home.shtml

NOTE: Must be a member AND have an appointment to shop.

FabScrap, See their website for pop-up shops at various locations and events and an online store: Brooklyn Army Terminal Building B, Unit 5H-4, 140 58th Street, Brooklyn, NY 11220

Tel: 929 276 3188

http://fabscrap.org

Big Reuse Brooklyn, 69 9th St Gowanus, NY 11215

Tel: 718 725 8925 Ext. 2

Email: brooklyn@bigreuse.org

www.bigreuse.org

Durham, North Carolina

The Scrap Exchange, Creative reuse arts center: 2050 Chapel Hill Road, Durham, NC 27707

Tel: 919 688 6960

http://scrapexchange.org

Scrap Thrift: 2020 Chapel Hill Road, Suite 31, Durham, NC 27707

Tel: 919 402 8989

http://scrapexchange.org

Toledo, Ohio

Scrap4Art: 33 West Wayne Street, Maumee, OH 43537

Tel: 419 720 2978

www.scrap4arttoledo.org

Eugene, Oregon

MECCA (Materials Exchange Center for Community Arts): 449 Willamette St, Eugene, OR 97401

Tel: 541 302 1810

Email: info@materials-exchange.org

www.materials-exchange.org

Portland, Oregon

Scrap PDX: 1736 SW Alder Street, Portland, OR 97205

Tel: 503 294 0769

https://scrappdx.org

Lancaster, Pennsylvania

Lancaster Creative Reuse: 1865 Lincoln Highway East, Lancaster, PA 17602

Tel: 717 617 2977

www.lancastercreativereuse.org

Philadelphia, Pennsylvania

Recycled Artist In Residency (RAIR): 7333 Milnor Street, Philadelphia, PA 19136

Email: Info@RAIRPHILLY.org

http://rairphilly.org

The Resource Exchange, Philadelphia creative reuse center: 1701 North 2nd Street, Philadelphia, PA 19122

Tel: 267 997 0060
Email: info@theresourceexchange.org
www.theresourceexchange.org

Philadelphia Recycling Co.: PO Box 4626, 3066 North 16th Street, Philadelphia, PA 19127

Tel: 215 990 4350
Email: info@philadelphiarecyclingcompany.com
www.philadelphiarecycling.co/materials

EForce Recycling: 3114 Grays Ferry Avenue, Philadelphia, PA 19146

Tel: 215 964 6665
Email: jay.segal@eforcecompliance.com
www.eforcerecycling.com

Providence, Rhode Island

Resources (Recycling) for R.I. Education: Spooner Street, Hathaway Center Suite 3, Providence, RI 12940

Tel: 401 781 1521
http://rrie.org

Nashville, Tennessee

SmART! Scrap Media ART Supplies!: 2416 Music Valley Drive, Suite 106, Nashville, TN 37214

Tel: 615 454 5808
www.smartsupplies.org

Turnip Green Creative Reuse: 945 Woodland St, Nashville, TN 37206

Tel: 615 720 7480
www.turnipgreencreativereuse.org

Houston, Texas

Texas Art Asylum: 1719 Live Oak, Houston, TX 77003

Tel: 713 224 5220
www.texasartasylum.com

Harrisonburg, Virginia

The Making Space: 620 Simms Avenue, Harrisonburg, VA 22802

Email: info.themakingspace@gmail.com

www.themakingspaceshenandoah.com or www.facebook.com/
theMakingSpaceShenandoah

Triphammer ReUse Center: 2255 N. Triphammer Road, Ithaca, NY
14850

https://ithacareuse.org

Seattle, Washington

Seattle ReCreative, A nonprofit organization dedicated to promoting
creativity, community, and environmental stewardship through creative
reuse and art education: 8408 Greenwood Ave North, Seattle, WA 98103

Tel: 206 297 1528

www.seattlerecreative.org

Washington, DC

Tanglewood Works, Where upcycling and art connect: 5132 Baltimore
Avenue, Hyattsville, MD 20781

https://tanglewoodworks.com

Upcycle, Creative Reuse Center (inside the Durant Arts Center): 1605
Cameron Street, Alexandria, VA 22314 (Metro: King Street)

Tel: 703 861 8705

www.upcyclecrc.org

Welton, Iowa

Make it Yours: 411 Main Street, Welton, IA 52774

Tel: 563 659 1534

www.makeityoursupcyclecenter.org

Create your own list here

_____

_____

_____

_____

_____

_____

_____

_____

_____

_____

_____

_____

_____

_____

_____

_____

_____

_____

_____

_____

_____

_____

_____

_____

Appendix 2

Customization considerations

We believe that almost any art activity could be used by and made interesting for nearly any audience. That does not mean we believe in a one size fits all! Before you use an art activity out of our book, or any book, you should always consider what changes you should make to best serve your audience. To that end, we have developed this checklist to help you tailor art directives for your audience. This list highlights a number of issues you may need to address when customizing an activity to best fit your participant(s).

Time: How much time do you have?

- How much time do you have for a project in a single session, group, or class? How much of the session, group, or class will be used for art making?

- Will the project need to be done in a single session or multiple sessions? Note that if your project spans multiple sessions, you may need to consider storage space for in-process projects.

- Will the participants continue to work on the project independently?

- Is there an opportunity for a display or publication that presents a deadline?

Space: What kind of space/venue do you have?

- Consider the size of your space, including how much moving around can be facilitated.

- What kind of space is it? You will use the space in a church basement or storefront very differently than you might use a hospital room or an interior school office.

- What are the features of the space?

  - What furniture is included and available in the room?

  - Does the space offer chalkboards, whiteboards, smart boards, bulletin boards, projection screens, poster board, tack strip, easels, podiums, pedestals, or other accessories that might be useful?

  - Are there privacy features? Inpatient day rooms may not have doors that close, or may have staff who require continuous access to the space.

- What are the parameters of the space?

  - Are there other people/groups who will be using the space before or after you? How long will you have for set-up and clean-up?

  - Can you rearrange the furniture to better accommodate your needs?

  - Are you able to make a mess, or to employ potentially messy materials in your space? What accommodations can be made in order to use messy materials? Do you need to use tarps to cover the floor, tables, or chairs?

  - Do you have access to water? A slop sink (i.e. janitorial sink) for easy clean-up? In a room without a sink, you might include a bucket of water or a container for collecting and then washing paint brushes.

- Is there noise pollution (e.g. televisions that remain on, P.A. system or intercoms, other groups or activities in the same room, music) or foot traffic?

Materials: What materials do you have?

- What directive or materials do you want to use, and why?

    - How does the material that you want to use link to your therapeutic treatment or educational goals?

    - How much experience do participants have with the given materials? Should you build in time for unstructured materials exploration?

    - Are there limitations presented by that material based on size, mess, budget, or storage needed?

- Are there any material restrictions for the facility you are working in or the population with which you are working? Examples of restrictions might include limitations for safety (e.g. no sharps), mess (e.g. no materials that leave a residue or that are easily carried throughout the facility), health or allergies (e.g. no toxic, smelly, or dusty materials)? Some institutions will now allow for the use of scissors, utility knives, oil paint, chalk pastel, clay, or glitter.

- What is your art materials budget?

    - What materials do you have that could substitute?

    - Do you have other projects or participants that will use the same materials?

    - Can you purchase in bulk to reduce cost per item? If so, is there a secure place to store the extra materials? Will it spoil if not used promptly?

- How much time can you spend scavenging materials?

    - Do you know of a place where they are easily accessible to you?

- Will materials need to be sorted or cleaned before use? Note that if you are using recycled materials, you should clean them thoroughly before use.

• How much art material storage do you have?

- For temporarily drying art projects?

- For longer-term storage of participant artwork?

• Is the storage space secure or shared? Remember that in art therapy, the art made in therapy is considered to be part of the clinical record, and should not be shared beyond the treating clinical team without the informed consent of the participant.

Client: Who is your participant? Who are you designing art activities for?

• Are you working with an individual or group?

- If a group, what is the relationship between group members?

- What session or stage is the group at?

- Is there a tension or cohesion between group members that you feel should be considered?

• What is the age and developmental stage of the participant(s)?

• Is there a presenting issue and/or diagnosis that should be considered?

- How will you keep an inventory of restricted materials to ensure they are not removed from a supervised environment?

• Does the participant have any specific strengths or weaknesses to consider? Preferences or aversions?

- What is the level of art experience, comfort, and proficiency in your participant?

  – In what ways can you provide the participant with some choice, agency, and autonomy?

- Is your participant willing to experiment and take risks?

  – If they are risk-averse, how will you pace the introduction of new materials and techniques?

- Are there any cultural connections or considerations participants may have with the project?

  How can you honor their existing knowledge or heritage?

- What is the level of trust built into your relationship with the participant?

  – How long have you been working together?

  – What session is this in the trajectory of your work together?

  – How long do you have left to continue working with this participant?

- What goal is your participant working on?

  – How does the project or material tie in with your participant's educational or therapeutic goals?

Outside influences: A variety of other circumstances may influence the way you customize activities that you facilitate

- Are there any cross-curricular expectations concerning educational or academic content?

- Are there specific assessment needs that must be met for the group, organization, state office, accrediting body, individual education plan or individual treatment plan (IEP/ITP)?

- Is there an expectation for final products worthy of display or publication?

- Is there feedback that is required or expected by administrators, grantors/funders, or family?

- Do you need to fulfill outsider requirements, such as those of a certifying or licensing body, grantors, or project sponsor?

Appendix 3

Books and recommended resources by project

Throughout our time exploring and researching for this book we have come across many terrific resources. For ease of reference we have listed a few of the stories, books, and websites here. Some of these sources contain exciting illustrations that will surely spark imagination. Others provide additional information to deepen the understanding of the origins of a certain project or theme. Still others offer a plethora of material concerning the specific traditions and rituals surrounding an art form we have shared. We believe that these resources can be helpful for use in your art and therapy groups to deepen the knowledge and promote understanding for your participants and yourself.

Masks: Vejigante masks

Deane, Z. (2018) 'The story behind the Vejigante mask of Puerto Rico.' Trip Savvy, March 11. Accessed on September 11, 2018 at www.tripsavvy.com/story-behind-the-vejigante-mask-of-puerto-rico-1622305

Delacre, L. (1993) *Vejigante Masquerader*. New York: Scholastic.

Foley, E. (1997) *Festivals of the World: Puerto Rico*. Milwaukee, WI: Gareth Stevens Publishing.

Fontanez, E. (1994) *The Vejigante and the Folk Festivals of Puerto Rico*. Arlington, VA: Exit Studio.

Loíza Aldea Yearly Patron Saints Day (n.d.) 'In the town of Loíza traditional activities…' Accessed on August 31, 2018 at www.elyunque.com/vejigante.htm

Our Story (n.d.) 'A Puerto Rican carnival.' Smithsonian's History Explorer. Accessed on August 31, 2018 at http://amhistory.si.edu/ourstory/activities/puerto

Wysochanski, J. (2017) 'Puerto Rican mask tradition to be featured in international festival parade.' Repeating Islands, June 9. Accessed on September 11, 2018 at https://repeatingislands.com/2017/06/09/puerto-rican-mask-tradition-to-be-featured-in-international-festival-parade

Flags: Tibetan Prayer Flags

Barker, D. (2003) *Tibetan Prayer Flags: Send Your Blessings on the Breeze [with Prayer Flags].* London, UK: Connections Book Publishing.

Beer, R. (2004) *Encyclopedia of Tibetan Symbols and Motifs.* Chicago, IL: Serindia Publications Inc.

Prayer Flag Project, The (2016) 'The Prayer Flag Project—A collective project spreading peace, good will and kindness, one flag at a time...' Blog, July 3. Accessed on September 11, 2018 at http://theprayerflagproject.blogspot.com

Radiant Heart (2014) 'Tibetan prayer flags and dharma banners from Radiant Heart.' Accessed on September 11, 2018 at www.prayerflags.com

Rubin Museum of Art, The (n.d.) 'DIY art-making: Tibetan prayer flags.' Accessed on September 11, 2018 at http://rubinmuseum.org/images/content/DIYArtmaking_ML4.pdf

Wise, T. (2002) *Blessings on the Wind: The Mystery and Meaning of Tibetan Prayer Flags.* San Francisco, CA: Chronicle Books.

Boxes: Fairy doors

Boyd, L. (2016) 'Fairy door: If you build it, fairies will come.' Blog post, June 6. Accessed on August 31, 2018 at www.leafcutterdesigns.com/blog/fairy-door-if-you-build-it

Boxes: Faux-stained glass windows

Hayward, J. (n.d.) 'Stained-glass windows: From *The New Book of Knowledge.*' Scholastic Art blog. Accessed on August 31, 2018 at www.scholastic.com/browse/article.jsp?id=3754175

Southwick, M. (2011) 'The oldest stained glass window in the world (NZ338652).' North-East History Tour blog, March 22. Accessed on September 3, 2018 at http://northeasthistorytour.blogspot.com/2011/03/oldest-stained-glass-window-in-world.html

Stained Glass Association of America (n.d.) http://stainedglass.org

Charms, talismans, amulets

Khamsas

Gomez, A. (1992) *Crafts of Many Cultures: 30 Authentic Craft Projects from Around the World*. New York: Scholastic Professional Books.

Yronwode, C. (n.d.) '*The Hamsa hand.*' *The "Lucky W" Amulet Archive*. Accessed on September 3, 2018 at www.luckymojo.com/hamsahand.html

Worry dolls

Brown, A. (2007) *Silly Billy*. London, UK: Walker Books Ltd.

Ferguson, J. (n.d.) 'Worry dolls.' Blog. Accessed on August 31, 2018 at www.tes.com/lessons/bgZrKZIM6QZMcg/worry-dolls

Kennedy, S. (2015) '*Muñecas quitapenas.*' Producing Polyglots blog, February 9. Accessed on August 31, 2018 at http://producingpolyglots.blogspot.com/2015/02/munecas-quitapenas.html

Port, B. (2014) 'Don't worry, be happy: Guatemalan worry dolls.' Uxibal blog, February 21. Accessed on September 3, 2018 at www.uxibal.com/dont-worry-be-happy-guatemalan-worry-dolls

Books and journals: Altered books

Attara, C. (2012) 'Healing loss through art…an altered book.' *Bereavement Care 31*(3), 136–139. doi:10.1080/02682621.2012.740297

Brazelton, B. (2004) *Altered Books Workshop: 18 Creative Techniques for Self-expression*. Cincinnati, OH: North Light Books.

Chilton, G. (2007) 'Altered books in art therapy with adolescents.' *Art Therapy: Journal of the American Art Therapy Association 24*(2), 59–63. doi:10.1080/07421656.2007.10129588

Harrison, H. (2002) *Altered Books, Collaborative Journals, and Other Adventures in Bookmaking*. Gloucester, MA: Rockport.

Huntley, E. (2015) 'Altered Book-making for Children and Adolescents Affected by Traumatic Loss.' Unpublished Master's thesis. Tallahassee, FL: Florida State University.

Vollrath, L. (2014) 'A crash course on altered books.' Mixed Media Club blog post, November 7. Accessed on September 3, 2018 at https://mixedmedia.club/a-crash-course-on-altered-books

References

Able Trust, The (2009) *Team Builders and Ice Breakers: Techniques for Success*. Accessed on August 31, 2018 at www.serviceandinclusion.org/conf/HSHT-Team-Building-Ice-Breaker-Manual-2008-09.pdf

Abrams, H.N. (1990) *Black Art: Ancestral Legacy: The African Impulse in African American Art*. Dallas, TX: Dallas Museum of Art.

Adams, A.J. (2009) 'Seeing is believing: The power of visualization.' Blog post, December 3. Accessed on August 31, 2018 at www.psychologytoday.com/us/blog/flourish/200912/seeing-is-believing-the-power-visualization

Agosin, M. (1996) *Tapestries of Hope, Threads of Love: The Arpillera Movement in Chile, 1974–1994* (translated by C. Kostopulos-Cooperman). Albuquerque, NM: University of New Mexico Press.

Agosin, M. (2014) *Stitching Resistance: Women, Creativity, and Fiber Arts*. Tunbridge Wells, UK: Solis Press.

Al-Banna, F. (2017) 'Recycling and artwork.' EcoMENA, June 4. Accessed on August 31, 2018 at www.ecomena.org/recycling-art

Anderson, L. (2010) *The Game Bible: Over 300 Games—the Rules, the Gear, the Strategies*. New York: Workman Publishing.

Art Story Contributors (2018) 'Earth art.' Accessed on August 31, 2018 at www.theartstory.org/movement-earth-art.htm

Asia Society (2018) 'Emakimono: Japanese picture scrolls.' Accessed on August 31, 2018 at https://asiasociety.org/education/emakimono

Barker, D. (2003) *Tibetan Prayer Flags: Send Your Blessings on the Breeze [with Prayer Flags]*. London, UK: Connections Book Publishing.

Beebe, A., Gelfand, E.W. and Bender, B. (2010) 'A randomized trial to test the effectiveness of art therapy for children with asthma.' *Journal of Allergy and Clinical Immunology 126*(2), 263–266. doi:10.1016/j.jaci.2010.03.019

Beer, R. (2004) *Encyclopedia of Tibetan Symbols and Motifs*. Chicago, IL: Serindia Publications Inc.

Bloom, S.L. (1997) *Creating Sanctuary: Toward the Evolution of Sane Societies*. New York: Routledge.

Bloom, S.L. (2004a) 'Neither liberty nor safety: The impact of fear on individuals, institutions, and societies, Part I.' *Psychotherapy and Politics International 2*(2), 78–98. doi:10.1002/ppi.75

Bloom, S.L. (2004b) 'Neither liberty nor safety: The impact of fear on individuals, institutions, and societies, Part II.' *Psychotherapy and Politics International 2*(3), 212–228.

Bloom, S.L. (2005) 'Neither liberty nor safety: The impact of fear on individuals, institutions, and societies, Part III.' *Psychotherapy and Politics International 3*(2), 96–111. doi:10.1002/ppi.23

Bloom, S.L. (2006) 'Neither liberty nor safety: The impact of fear on individuals, institutions, and societies, Part IV.' *Psychotherapy and Politics International 4*(1), 4–23. doi:10.1002/ppi.34

Bolwerk, A., Mack-Andrick, J., Lang, F.R., Dörfler, A. and Maihöfner, C. (2014) 'How art changes your brain: Differential effects of visual art production and cognitive art evaluation on functional brain connectivity.' *PLOS One 9*(7). doi:10.1371/journal.pone.0101035

Boyd, L. (2016) 'Fairy door: If you build it, fairies will come.' Blog post, June 6. Accessed on August 31, 2018 at www.leafcutterdesigns.com/blog/fairy-door-if-you-build-it

Breathe Network, The (n.d.) 'Creating safer spaces for healing sexual violence: An interview with Tovah Means.' Blog post. Accessed on June 18, 2018 at www.thebreathenetwork.org/creating-safe-spaces-for-healing-sexual-violence-an-interview-with-tovah-means

Brown, A. (2007) *Silly Billy*. London, UK: Walker Books Ltd.

Brumleve, E. (n.d.) 'Expressive mask making for teens: Beginning insights.' American Art Therapy Association, Inc. Accessed on August 31, 2018 at www.arttherapy.org/upload/News&Info/ExpressiveMaskMakingForTeens.pdf

Burke, P. (2005) *The Historical Anthropology of Early Modern Italy: Essays on Perception and Communication*. Cambridge, UK: Cambridge University Press.

Buchalter, S. (2009) *Art Therapy Techniques and Applications: A Model for Practice*. London, UK: Jessica Kingsley Publishers.

Buchalter, S. (2011) *Art Therapy and Creative Coping Techniques for Older Adults*. London, UK: Jessica Kingsley Publishers.

Buchalter, S.I. (2015) *Raising Self-esteem in Adults: An Eclectic Approach with Art Therapy, CBT and DBT based Techniques*. London, UK: Jessica Kingsley Publishers.

CAEA (Center for Art of East Asia, University of Chicago) (2018) 'East Asian scroll paintings.' Accessed on August 31, 2018 at https://scrolls.uchicago.edu

Callaway, E. (n.d.) 'The art of recycling.' Groundwork. Accessed on August 31, 2018 at www.groundworkpresents.com/the-art-of-recycling

Carlson, L. (1994) *More than Moccasins*. Chicago, IL: Chicago Review Press.

Cavendish, M. (1975) 'Popup cards & fan folds.' In *The Complete Encyclopedia of Crafts* (Vol. 1). New York: Columbia House.

Chapman, L.M., Morabito, D., Ladakakos, C., Schreier, H. and Knudson, M.M. (2001) 'The effectiveness of art therapy interventions in reducing Post Traumatic Stress Disorder (PTSD) symptoms in pediatric trauma patients.' *Art Therapy: Journal of the American Art Therapy Association 18*(2), 100–104.

Charland, W. (2011) 'War rugs: Woven documents of conflict and hope.' *Art Education 64*(6), 25–32.

Chilton, G. (2007) 'Altered books in art therapy with adolescents.' *Art Therapy: Journal of the American Art Therapy Association 24*(2), 59–63. doi:10.1080/07421656.2007.10129588

Chilton, G. (2013) 'Altered inquiry: Discovering arts-based research through an altered book.' *The International Journal of Qualitative Methods 12*(1), 457–477. doi:10.1177/160940691301200123

Chu, V. (2010) 'Within the box: Cross-cultural art therapy with survivors of the Rwanda genocide.' *Art Therapy: Journal of the American Art Therapy Association* 27(1), 4–10.

Cicione, R.M., Fontaine, L.A. and Williams, C.N. (2002) 'Trauma Relief Unlimited: An outcome study of a new treatment method.' *Trauma and Loss: Research and Interventions* 2(2), 25–33.

Ciornai, S. and Ruiz, M.C. (2016) 'Latin American Art Therapy: Collective Dreams and Horizons of Hope.' In D.E. Gussak and M.L. Rosal (eds) *The Wiley Handbook of Art Therapy* (pp.753–764). Somerset, NJ: John Wiley & Sons.

Cobb, R.A. and Negash, S. (2010) 'Altered book making as a form of art therapy: A narrative approach.' *Journal of Family Psychotherapy* 21(1), 54–69. doi:10.1080/08975351003618601

Cohen, B.M. and Cox, C.T. (1995) *Telling without Talking: Art as a Window into the World of Multiple Personality.* New York: W.W. Norton & Company.

Cohen, R.A. (2013) 'Common threads: A recovery programme for survivors of gender-based violence.' *Intervention: Journal of Mental Health and Psychosocial Support in Conflict Affected Areas* 11(2), 157–168.

Coholic, D. (2010) *Arts Activities for Children and Young People in Need: Helping Children to Develop Mindfulness, Spiritual Awareness and Self-esteem.* London, UK: Jessica Kingsley Publishers.

Comas-Díaz, L. and Jansen, M.A. (1995) 'Global conflict and violence against women.' *Peace & Conflict* 1(4), 315.

Corrington, D.R. (2012) 'Outside/inside masks.' Art Therapy: Sharing Directives blog, August 9. Accessed on August 31, 2018 at http://arttherapydirectives.blogspot.com/2012/08/outsideinside-masks.html

Creative Growth (n.d.) 'Judith Scott.' Accessed on August 31, 2018 at www.creativegrowth.org/artists/judith-scott

Crenshaw, D.A. and Green, E.J. (2009) 'The symbolism of windows and doors in play therapy.' *Play Therapy Magazine*, 6–8.

Cruz, E. (2014, July 25) 'Exploring faith, sexuality, and safe spaces through film and art.' Advocate, July 25. Accessed on August 31, 2018 at www.advocate.com/politics/religion/2014/07/25/exploring-faith-sexuality-and-safe-spaces-through-film-and-art

Dall, W.H. (1884) 'On masks, labrets, and certain aboriginal customs, with an inquiry into the bearing of their geographical distribution.' *Bureau of American Ethnology, Annual Report 3*, 73–151. Washington, DC: US Government Printing Office [Reprinted 2010].

Delbanco, D. (2008) 'Chinese handscrolls.' The Met. Accessed on August 31, 2018 at www.metmuseum.org/toah/hd/chhs/hd_chhs.htm

Dunn-Snow, P. and Joy-Smellie, S. (2011) 'Teaching art therapy techniques: Mask-making, a case in point.' *Art Therapy: Journal of the American Art Therapy Association* 17(2), 125–131. doi:10.1080/07421656.2000.10129512

Erikson, E. (1980) *Childhood and Society* (4th edn). New York: W.W. Norton.

Falcon, A. (n.d.) 'Recycled art: 66 masterpieces made from junk.' Hongkiat, Artwork blog post. Accessed on August 31, 2018 at www.hongkiat.com/blog/recycled-art-masterpiece-made-from-junks

Farrell-Kirk, R. (2001) 'Secrets, symbols, synthesis, and safety: The role of boxes in art therapy.' *American Journal of Art Therapy* 39(3), 88–92.

Feen-Calligan, H., McIntyre, B. and Sands-Goldstein, M. (2009) 'Art therapy applications of dolls in grief recovery, identity and community service.' *Art Therapy: Journal of the American Art Therapy Association 26*(4), 167–173. doi:10.1 080/07421656.2009.10129613

Ferguson, J. (n.d.) 'Worry dolls.' Blog. Accessed on August 31, 2018 at www.tes.com/lessons/bgZrKZIM6QZMcg/worry-dolls

Flag of Puerto Rico, The (n.d.) Accessed on August 31, 2018 at www.topuertorico.org/reference/flag.shtml

Frank, A. (2017) 'Helping clients build their life rafts.' Counseling Today blog post, June 5. Accessed on August 31, 2018 at https://ct.counseling.org/2017/06/helping-clients-build-life-rafts

Fry, G. (1990) *Stitched from the Soul: Slave Quilts from the Antebellum South.* Chapel Hill, NC: University of North Carolina Press.

Gantt, L. and Tinnin, L.W. (2007) 'Intensive trauma therapy of PTSD and dissociation: An outcome study.' *The Arts in Psychotherapy 34*(1), 68–80. doi:10.1016/j.aip.2006.09.007

Geue, K., Goetze, H., Buttstaedt, M., Kleinert, E., Richter, D. and Singer, S. (2010) 'An overview of art therapy interventions for cancer patients and the results of research.' *Complementary Therapies in Medicine 18,* 160–170. doi:10.1016/j.ctim.2010.04.001

Goldberg, R.M. and Stephenson, J.B. (2016) 'Staying with the metaphor: Applying reality therapy's use of metaphors to grief counseling.' *Journal of Creativity in Mental Health 11*(1), 105–117. doi:10.1080/15401383.2015.1113396

Goldsworthy, A. (2015) *Andy Goldsworthy: Ephemeral Works: 2004–2014.* New York: Harry N. Abrams.

Gomez, A. (1992) *Crafts of Many Cultures: 30 Authentic Craft Projects from Around the World.* New York: Scholastic Professional Books.

Guest, J. (2017) *The Art Activity Book for Relational Work: 100 Illustrated Therapeutic Worksheets to Use with Individuals, Couples and Families.* London, UK: Jessica Kingsley Publishers.

Hanoch, D. (2016) 'The art of focusing: How to practice object meditation.' Blog post, September 20. Accessed on August 31, 2018 at https://beyogi.com/the-art-of-focusing-how-to-practice-object-meditation

Hargrave-Nykaza, K. (1994) 'An application of art therapy to the trauma of rape.' *Art Therapy: Journal of the American Art Therapy Association 11*(1), 53–57. doi:10.108 0/07421656.1994.10759044

Hayward, J. (n.d.) 'Stained-glass windows: from *The New Book of Knowledge.*' Scholastic Art blog. Accessed on August 31, 2018 at www.scholastic.com/browse/article.jsp?id=3754175

Howcast (2009) 'How to make a paper-mache mask.' YouTube video, September 16. Accessed on August 31, 2018 at www.youtube.com/watch?v=FCiYNE_hmNg&feature=youtu.be

Hrenko, K.D. (2005) 'Remembering camp dreamcatcher: Art therapy with children whose lives have been touched by HIV/AIDS.' *Art Therapy: Journal of the American Art Therapy Association 22*(1), 39–43.

Jackson, L., Mezzera, C. and Satterberg, M. (2017) 'Wisdom through Diversity in Art Therapy.' In R. Carolan and A. Backos (eds) *Emerging Perspectives in Art Therapy: Trends, Movements, and Developments* (pp.1–3). Abingdon, UK: Routledge.

Johnson, D.R. (1987) 'The role of the creative arts therapies in diagnosis and treatment of psychological trauma.' *The Arts in Psychotherapy 14*, 7–13.

Johnson, J.H. (2011) *Venice Incognito: Masks in the Serene Republic.* Berkeley, CA: University of California Press.

Jones, D.N. (2018) 'Walkabout: FOCUS Pittsburgh trauma recovery model drawing national attention.' *Pittsburgh Post-Gazette,* June 18. Accessed on August 31, 2018 at www.post-gazette.com/opinion/diana-nelson-jones/2018/06/18/Local-trauma-recovery-model-drawing-national-attention/stories/201806170065

Jones, K. (2013) 'Seeing the art in plastic straws and other castoffs.' *New York Times,* March 20. Accessed on August 31, 2018 at www.nytimes.com/2013/03/21/arts/artsspecial/students-use-recycled-materials-to-create-art.html

Kaimal, G. (2017, February 16) 'Unmasking the trauma: A look at research on mask making as a creative arts therapy.' National Endowment for the Arts: Art works blog post, February 16. Accessed on August 31, 2018 at www.arts.gov/art-works/2017/unmasking-trauma-look-research-mask-making-creative-arts-therapy

Karabanow, J. and Naylor, T. (2015) 'Using art to tell stories and build safe spaces: Transforming academic research into action.' *Canadian Journal of Community Mental Health 34*(3), 67–85. doi:10.7870/cjcmh-2015-005

Kaufman, A.B. (1996) 'Art in boxes: An exploration in meaning.' *The Arts in Psychotherapy 3*(3), 237–247.

Kennedy, S. (2015) '*Muñecas quitapenas.*' Producing Polyglots blog post, February 9. Accessed on August 31, 2018 at http://producingpolyglots.blogspot.com/2015/02/munecas-quitapenas.html

Klammer, S. (n.d.) '100 art therapy exercises: The updated and improved list.' Expressive Art Inspirations blog post. Accessed on August 31, 2018 at http://intuitivecreativity.typepad.com/expressiveartinspirations/100-art-therapy-exercises.html

Knight, C. (2016) 'Identity transformed in the Fowler's "Disguise: Masks and Global African Art".' Los Angeles Times, January 27. Accessed on August 31, 2018 at www.latimes.com/entertainment/arts/la-et-cm-disguise-masks-fowler-review-20160128-column.html

Kordic, A. (2016) 'Assemblage artists who taunt the mood and perception.' Wide Walls, May 16. Accessed on August 31, 2018 at www.widewalls.ch/assemblage-artists

Kouyoumdjian, H., Zamboanga, B.L. and Hansen, D.J. (2003) 'Barriers to community mental health services for Latinos: Treatment considerations.' *Clinical Psychology: Science and Practice 10*(4), 394–422.

Kramer, E. (1971) *Art as Therapy with Children.* New York: Schocken Books.

Kraybill, O.G. (2018) 'Trauma processing: When and when not?' Psychology Today blog post, April 11. Accessed on August 31, 2018 at www.psychologytoday.com/us/blog/expressive-trauma-integration/201804/trauma-processing-when-and-when-not

Lahad, M., Farhi, M., Leykin, D. and Kaplansky, N. (2010) 'Preliminary study of a new integrative approach in treating post-traumatic stress disorder: SEE FAR CBT.' *The Arts in Psychotherapy 37*(5), 391–399. doi:10.1016/j.aip.2010.07.003

Landgarten, H.B. (1981) *Clinical Art Therapy: A Comprehensive Guide.* New York: Routledge.

Leasure, T. (2017) 'Art therapy: 15 activities and exercises for children and adults.' Positive Psychology Program blog post, December 7. Accessed on August 31, 2018 at https://positivepsychologyprogram.com/art-therapy

Leckey, J. (2011) 'The therapeutic effectiveness of creative activities on mental well-being: A systematic review of the literature.' *Journal of Psychiatric and Mental Health Nursing 18*(6), 501–509. doi:10.1111/j.1365-2850.2011.01693.x

Liebmann, M. (1986) *Art Therapy for Groups: A Handbook of Themes and Exercises* (2nd edn). New York: Brunner-Routledge.

Linesch, D., Metzel, E. and Trevino, A.L. (2016) 'Various Aspects of Art Therapy in Mexico/Algunos Aspectos de la Terapia de Arte en Mexico.' In D.E. Gussak and M.L. Rosal (eds) *The Wiley Handbook of Art Therapy* (pp.745–752). Somerset, NJ: John Wiley & Sons.

Loíza Aldea Yearly Patron Saints Day (n.d.) 'In the town of Loíza traditional activities…' Accessed on August 31, 2018 at www.elyunque.com/vejigante.htm

Luckett, K. (2011) 'Art journaling.' Blog post, November 25. Accessed on August 31, 2018 at http://artjournaling.blogspot.com

Lyshak-Stelzer, F., Singer, P., St John, P. and Chemtob, C.M. (2007) 'Art therapy for adolescents with Posttraumatic Stress Disorder symptoms: A pilot study.' *Art Therapy: Journal of the American Art Therapy Association 24*(4), 163–169. doi:10.1 080/07421656.2007.10129474

MacKenzie, S. (2015) 'Symbolism on doors.' Blog post, July 5. Accessed on August 31, 2018 at https://breathofgreenair.com/2015/07/05/symbolism-of-doors

Makin, S.R. (2000) *Therapeutic Art Directives and Resources: Activities and Initiatives for Individuals and Groups.* London, UK: Jessica Kingsley Publishers.

Malone, S.N. and Rosal, M.L. (1993) 'Journey toward integration: The use of collages to assess the separation and individuation process as an adult identical twin.' *Art Therapy: Journal of the American Art Therapy Association 10*(1), 16–22.

Maslow, A.H. (1943) 'A theory of human motivation.' *Psychological Review 50*(4), 370–96. doi:10.1037/h0054346

McCarthy, M. (2010) 'Identity parade: What do flags say about nations and human nature?' Independent, April 23. Accessed on August 31, 2018 at www.independent.co.uk/news/uk/this-britain/identity-parade-what-do-flags-say-about-nations-ndash-and-human-nature-1951698.html

Miller, G. (2011) 'Prayer flag making begins.' Creativity in Motion blog post, August 27. Accessed on August 31, 2018 at https://gretchenmiller.wordpress.com/2011/08/27/prayer-flag-making-begins

Millington, R. (2017) 'Art history: Cultural appropriation & the art of the steal.' Blog post, May 8. Accessed on August 31, 2018 at http://ruthmillington.co.uk/the-art-of-the-steal-cultural-appropriation-art-history

Mok, K. (2009) 'Top 5 environmental artists shaking up the art world.' Treehugger blog post, February 18. Accessed on August 31, 2018 at www.treehugger.com/culture/top-5-environmental-artists-shaking-up-the-art-world.html

Moon, C.H. (2011) *Materials and Media in Art Therapy: Critical Understandings of Diverse Artistic Vocabularies.* New York: Routledge.

Morgan, J. (2001) 'Boxes and remembering in the time of Aids.' *AIDS Bulletin 10*(2), 17–20.

Moya-Raggio, E. (1984) '"Arpilleras": Chilean culture of resistance.' *Feminist Studies 10*(2), 277–290. doi:10.2307/3177867

Narrative Therapy Centre (n.d.) 'About narrative therapy.' Accessed on August 31, 2018 at www.narrativetherapycentre.com/narrative.html

National Museum of Women in the Arts (n.d.) 'Louise Nevelson.' Accessed on August 31, 2018 at https://nmwa.org/explore/artist-profiles/louise-nevelson

Nicolas, K. (2015) 'Art-ed: Artists working with natural materials.' Blog post, August 20. Accessed on August 31, 2018 at http://blog.indiewalls.com/2015/08/art-ed-top-7-artists-working-with-natural-materials

Ochberg, F.M. (1991) 'Post-traumatic therapy.' *Psychotherapy: Theory, Research, Practice, Training 28*(1), 5–15. doi:10.1037/0033-3204.28.1.5

Peacock, M.E. (1991) 'A personal construct approach to art therapy in the treatment of post sexual abuse trauma.' *American Journal of Art Therapy 29*, 100–109.

Pennebaker, J.W. and Smyth, J.M. (2016) *Opening Up By Writing It Down.* New York: The Guilford Press.

Piaget, J. (1951) *Play, Dreams, and Imitation in Childhood* (translated by C. Gattegno and F. Hodgson). New York: W.W. Norton.

Pifalo, T. (2007) 'Jogging the cogs: Trauma-focused art therapy and cognitive behavioral therapy with sexually abused children.' *Art Therapy: Journal of the American Art Therapy Association 24*(4), 170–175.

Port, B. (2014) 'Don't worry, be happy: Guatemalan worry dolls.' Uxibal blog post, February 21. Accessed on September 3, 2018 at www.uxibal.com/dont-worry-be-happy-guatemalan-worry-dolls

Potash, J.S., Doby-Copeland, C., Stepney, S.A., Washington, B.N. *et al.* (2015) 'Advancing multicultural and diversity competence in art therapy: American Art Therapy Association Multicultural Committee 1990–2015.' *Art Therapy 32*(3), 146–150. doi:10.1080/07421656.2015.1060837

Prayer Flag Project, The (2016) 'The Prayer Flag Project—A collective project spreading peace, good will and kindness, one flag at a time…' Blog, July 3. Accessed on September 11, 2018 at http://theprayerflagproject.blogspot.com

Puetz, T.W., Morley, C.A. and Herring, M.P. (2013) 'Effects of creative arts therapies on psychological symptoms and quality of life in patients with cancer.' *Journal of the American Medical Association: Internal Medicine 173*(11), 960–969. doi:10.1001/jamainternmed.2013.836

Puig, A., Lee, S.M., Goodwin, L. and Sherrard, P.A.D. (2006) 'The efficacy of creative arts therapies to enhance emotional expression, spirituality, and psychological well-being of newly diagnosed stage I and stage II breast cancer patients: A preliminary study.' *The Arts in Psychotherapy 33*(3), 218–228. doi:10.1016/j.aip.2006.02.004

Radiant Heart Studios (2014) 'Tibetan prayer flags and dharma banners from Radiant Heart.' Accessed on September 3, 2018 at www.prayerflags.com

Raffaelli, T. and Hartzell, E. (2016) 'A comparison of adults' responses to collage versus drawing in an initial art-making session.' *Art Therapy: Journal of the American Art Therapy Association 33*(1), 21–26. doi:10.1080/07421656.2016.1127115

Rappaport, L. (1998) 'Focusing and art therapy: Tools for working through post-traumatic stress disorder.' *Focusing Folio 17*(1). Accessed on September 3, 2018 at www.focusing.org/pdf/rappaport_focusing_and_art_therapy_tools_for_working_through_trauma.pdf

Rappaport, L. (2009) *Focusing-oriented Art Therapy: Accessing the Body's Wisdom and Creative Intelligence.* London, UK: Jessica Kingsley Publishers.

Reiter, M.D. (2017) *Family Therapy: An Introduction to Process, Practice and Theory.* New York: Routledge.

Reiter, S. (2009) *Writing away the Demons: Stories of Creative Coping through Transformative Writing.* Clearwater, MN: North Star Press of St Cloud.

Reiter, S. (2016) 'Transformative writing.' The Creative Writing Center, May 2. Accessed on September 3, 2018 at http://sherryreiter.blogspot.com/2016/05/transformative-writing.html

Reyes Berry, C. (1982) 'Getting started in box lining.' *Decorating & Craft Ideas,13*(4). Richard M. Fontana, Jr, Publisher.

Reynolds, F. (2000) 'Managing depression through needlecraft creative activities: A qualitative study.' *Arts in Psychotherapy 27*(2), 107–114.

Reynolds, F. (2004) 'Conversations about creativity and chronic illness II: Textile artists coping with long-term health problems reflect on the creative process.' *Creativity Research Journal 16*(1), 79–89. doi:10.1207/s15326934crj1601

Rubin, L.C. (2008) 'Even Superheroes Have Problems.' In L. Lowenstein (ed.) *Assessment and Treatment Activities for Children, Adolescents, and Families: Practitioners Share Their Most Effective Techniques* (pp.154–155). Toronto, ON: Champion Press.

Rubin Museum of Art, The (n.d.) 'DIY art-making: Tibetan prayer flags.' Accessed on September 11, 2018 at http://rubinmuseum.org/images/content/DIYArtmaking_ML4.pdf

Schreier, H., Ladakakos, C., Morabito, D., Chapman, L. and Knudson, M.M. (2005) 'Posttraumatic stress symptoms in children after mild to moderate pediatric trauma: A longitudinal examination of symptom prevalence, correlates, and parent-child symptom reporting.' *Journal of Trauma-Injury Infection & Critical Care 58*(2), 353–363. doi:10.1097/01.TA.0000152537.15672.B7

Schwartz, D. (n.d.) 'Unmasked—Expressive arts therapy directive.' Art Therapy blog post. Retrieved from www.arttherapyblog.com/art-therapy-activities/unmasked

Seltzer, W. (2008) *Craft: Transforming Traditional Crafts. Vol. 6*. Sebastopol, CA: O'Reilly Media.

Sethre, J. (2003) *The Souls of Venice*. Jefferson, NC: McFarland.

Southwick, M. (2011) 'The oldest stained glass window in the world (NZ338652).' North-East History Tour blog post, March 22. Accessed on September 3, 2018 at http://northeasthistorytour.blogspot.com/2011/03/oldest-stained-glass-window-in-world.html

Squire, C. (1996) 'The Open Closing Door: Impossible Theatre's Video Art Work with Offenders, Victims and Observers of Crime.' In M. Liebmann (ed.) *Arts Approaches to Conflict* (pp.347–368). London, UK: Jessica Kingsley Publishers.

Stonebarger, A. (n.d.) 'Guide to Russian lacquer boxes.' Accessed on September 3, 2018 at www.tradestonegallery.com/index.php?content=boxguide

Strauss, A. (2015) 'Treading the ground of contested memory: Archivists and the human rights movement in Chile.' *Archival Science 15*, 369–397. doi:10.1007/s10502-014-9223-3

Stuckey, H.L. and Nobel, J. (2010) 'The connection between art, healing, and public health: A review of current literature.' *American Journal of Public Health 100*(2), 254–263. doi:10.2105/AJPH.2008.156497

Svensk, A.C., Oster, I., Thyme, K.E., Magnusson, E. *et al.* (2009) 'Art therapy improves experienced quality of life among women undergoing treatment for breast cancer: A randomized controlled study.' *European Journal of Cancer Care 18*(1), 69–77.

Swank, J.M. (2008) 'Positive Postings.' In L. Lowenstein (ed.) *Assessment and Treatment Activities for Children, Adolescents, and Families: Practitioners Share Their Most Effective Techniques* (pp.164–165). Toronto, ON: Champion Press.

Tanap, R. (2017) 'Mindful: Exploring mental health through art.' NAMI (National Alliance on Mental Illness) blog post, January 13. Accessed on September 3, 2018 at www.nami.org/Blogs/NAMI-Blog/January-2017/Mindful-Exploring-Mental-Health-Through-Art

Thorpe, A. (2017) 'Equality and diversity—Do we really know who's engaging?' A New Direction blog post, April 5. Accessed on September 3, 2018 at www.anewdirection.org.uk/blog/equality-and-diversity-do-we-really-know-whos-engaging

Vollrath, L. (2014) 'A crash course on altered books.' Mixed Media Club blog post, November 7. Accessed on September 3, 2018 at https://mixedmedia.club/a-crash-course-on-altered-books

Wadeson, H. (2000) *Art Therapy Practice: Innovative Approaches with Diverse Populations.* Hoboken, NJ: Wiley.

Walker, M.S., Kaimal, G., Gonzaga, A.M.L., Myers-Coffman, K.A. and Degraba, T.J. (2017) 'Active-duty military service members' visual representations of PTSD and TBI in masks.' *International Journal of Qualitative Studies on Health and Well-being* *12*(1). doi:10.1080/17482631.2016.1267317

Waller, D. (2014) *Group Interactive Art Therapy: Its Use in Training and Treatment.* London, UK: Routledge.

Webster, G. (2012) 'The eco artists turning trash into treasure.' CNN, March 16. Accessed on September 3, 2018 at www.cnn.com/2012/03/16/world/environmental-green-art/index.html

Werker, K.P. (2014) *Make It Mighty Ugly: Exercises and Advice for Getting Creative Even When It Ain't Pretty.* Seattle, WA: Sasquatch Books.

White, M. and Epston, D. (1990) *Narrative Means to Therapeutic Ends.* New York: W.W. Norton & Company.

Winnicott, D.W. (1965) 'Ego Distortion in Terms of True and False Self.' In D.W. Winnicott (ed.) *The Maturational Process and the Facilitating Environment: Studies in the Theory of Emotional Development* (pp.140–152). London, UK: Hogarth Press [Original work published in 1960].

Winnicott, D.W. (1975) 'Anxiety Associated with Insecurity.' In D.W. Winnicott (ed.) *Through Paediatrics to Psycho-analysis* (pp.97–100). New York: Basic Books [Original work published in 1952].

Wise, T. (2002) *Blessings on the Wind: The Mystery and Meaning of Tibetan Prayer Flags.* San Francisco, CA: Chronicle Books.

Yates, M. and Pawley, K. (1987) 'Utilizing imagery and the unconscious to explore and resolve the trauma of sexual abuse.' *Art Therapy: Journal of the American Art Therapy Association 4*(1), 36–41. doi:10.1080/07421656.1987.10758697

Youngs, C. (2010) *Papercrafting in No Time: 50 Inspirational Projects Crafted from Paper.* London, UK: CICO Books.

Yronwode, C. (n.d.) 'The Hamsa hand. The "Lucky W" Amulet Archive.' Accessed on September 3, 2018 at www.luckymojo.com/hamsahand.html

Zella, C. (2017) 'Creating connections with nature via art.' Huffpost blog post, December 6. Accessed on September 3, 2018 at www.huffingtonpost.com/carmen-zella/creating-connections-withland-art_b_4833677.html

Zwicky, C. (2010) 'The masks we wear: Identity, art, and AIDS.' Inside Out: A MoMA/MoMA PS1 blog post, March 1. Accessed on September 3, 2018 at www.moma.org/explore/inside_out/2010/03/01/the-masks-we-wear-identity-art-and-aids

Index